Guide to Spitsbergen

Sam Gardener

Guide to Spitsbergen

Andreas Umbreit

BRADT PUBLICATIONS, UK
HUNTER PUBLISHING, USA

First published in 1991 by Bradt Publications, 41 Nortoft
Road, Chalfont St Peter, Bucks, SL9 0LA, England.
Distributed in the USA by Hunter Publishing Inc., 300
Raritan Center Parkway, CN94, Edison, NJ 08810.

British Library Cataloguing in Publication Data
Umbreit, Andreas
    Guide to Spitsbergen.
    1.Norway. Spitzbergen. Visitors' guides
    I. Title II. Spitzbergen Reisehandbuch. English
    919.8104

    ISBN 0-946983-33-X

Translated from the German by Wendy Lubetkin and
Gisela Gschaider, edited by Carolyn Walton

Photos by Andreas Umbreit unless otherwise stated
Maps by Andreas Umbreit and Caroline Crump
Front cover photo by Simon Fraser
Typeset from disc by Patti Taylor, London NW8 0RJ
Printed by Guernsey Press, Channel Islands

Acknowledgments

Special Thanks to the Sysselmann Mr Leif Eldring and to Mr Magnus Sturhaug of SNSK for the interviews granted, and the valuable information they provided. Thanks also to the office of the Sysselmann and to Mr Ian Gjerts (Nature Conservancy warden of Svalbard and member of the Norsk Polarinstitutt) who read through the original German manuscript.

The publisher thanks Mark Cowardine and Noel Cairns for checking the English text.

About the Author

Andreas Umbreit was born in 1959 in Munich and grew up in the Bavarian Alps, close to the Austrian border. Following his military service, his studies in agricultural science took him to Kiel on the Baltic.

In addition to hiking in the Alps of his homeland he discovered his love for the north, whilst still a schoolboy, during a month's tour of Scotland.

On later walking holidays he explored Scandinavia and travelled to Spitsbergen where he now runs a business organising trekking tours. This Arctic archipelago has completely enchanted him, not just the islands' wildlife, but also its people and their way of life. One reason for writing this book was his desire to provide detailed information for visitors who intend to come to this part of the world, and to avoid the conflicts arising from the inconsiderate behaviour of ill-informed tourists.

Preface

Only about 22,000 people visit Spitsbergen each year. The Norwegian administration only wants a modest opening to tourism since it hopes to protect the Arctic from the consequences of mass tourism.

At present, however, Norway is confronted with the problem that Spitsbergen's communities which rely on coal can only be maintained by state subsidy. The cautious development of controlled tourism is thus a way of reducing the islands' need for subsidies.

At the moment, the visitor to Spitsbergen, who has been courted for his wallet in other lands, finds himself in the unaccustomed situation that tourism is seen as an unavoidable development that should not be allowed to turn into a mass business.

The visitor must be aware of Norway's endeavour to minimize the negative side effects of tourism, on the environment and on taxpayers, and understand the necessity of certain rules. These include protective precautions for the wildlife, registration of all tour groups, and the requirement of self defence weapons and other adequate equipment.

I would like to express my hope that Norway will continue to maintain Spitsbergen unspoiled. The visitor should appreciate this remarkable achievement and support the authorities here through his own cooperative behaviour.

Andreas Umbreit
Dammstr. 36
D- 2300 Kiel 1
West Germany
Tel 0431 91678

Kiel, February 1990

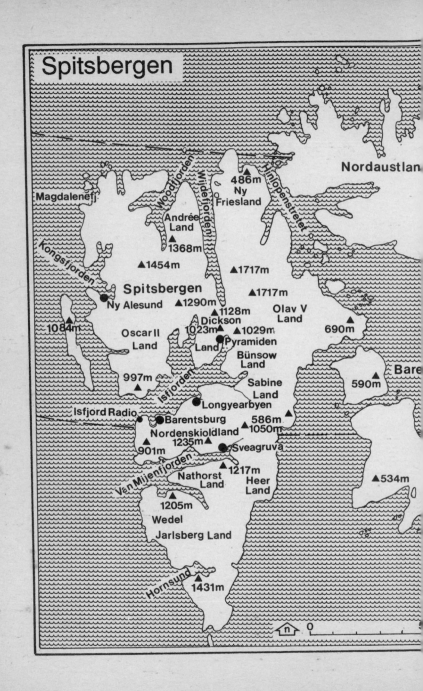

Spitsbergen

Nordaustlan...

Magdalenefj.

Woodfjorden

Wijdefjorden

Hinlopenstretet

486m
Ny
Friesland

Andrée
Land

1368m

Kongsfjorden

▲1454m

▲1717m

Spitsbergen

▲1717m

Ny Alesund

▲1290m

Olav V
Land

▲1128m
Dickson
1023m▲ ▲1029m
Land   Pyramiden

690m

▲
1084m

Oscar II
Land

Bünsow
Land

Bare

Isfjorden

Sabine
Land

590m

997m
▲

Longyearbyen

Isfjord Radio

586m
▲1050m

Barentsburg
Nordenskioldland
1235m▲

▲
901m

Sveagruva

Van Mijenfjorden

▲1217m

Nathorst
Land

Heer
Land

▲534m

▲
1205m

Wedel
Jarlsberg Land

Hornsund

▲1431m

n   0

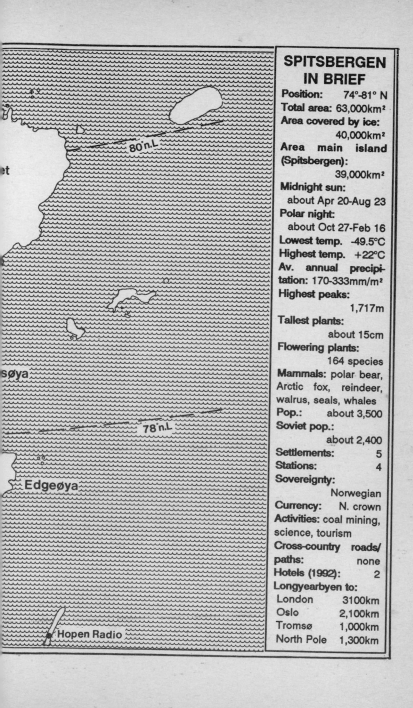

80°n.L

et

søya

78°n.L

Edgeøya

Hopen Radio

SPITSBERGEN IN BRIEF

Position:	74°-81° N
Total area:	63,000km²
Area covered by ice:	40,000km²
Area main island (Spitsbergen):	39,000km²
Midnight sun:	about Apr 20-Aug 23
Polar night:	about Oct 27-Feb 16
Lowest temp.	-49.5°C
Highest temp.	+22°C
Av. annual precipitation:	170-333mm/m²
Highest peaks:	1,717m
Tallest plants:	about 15cm
Flowering plants:	164 species
Mammals:	polar bear, Arctic fox, reindeer, walrus, seals, whales
Pop.:	about 3,500
Soviet pop.:	about 2,400
Settlements:	5
Stations:	4
Sovereignty:	Norwegian
Currency:	N. crown
Activities:	coal mining, science, tourism
Cross-country roads/paths:	none
Hotels (1992):	2

Longyearbyen to:

London	3100km
Oslo	2,100km
Tromsø	1,000km
North Pole	1,300km

TABLE OF CONTENTS

The Svalbard poppy, symbol of the short Arctic summer

INTRODUCTION

The official Norwegian name for the archipelago, including Bear Island, is Svalbard. Generally, however, it is known by its more common name Spitsbergen.

One of the special charms of Spitsbergen, an area nearly as big as the Republic of Ireland, is that it is almost totally unspoiled. With a total population of about 3,500 inhabitants in its five small settlements, and about 1,000 visitors (scientists and tourists) each year who stay for five or more days, there is enough space to be able to spend days, even weeks in the countryside without meeting anyone. The majority of the 22,000 tourists who come to the islands by cruise ship or night-charter flight only spend a few hours or days here. The moment you leave one of the settlements you are completely on your own and must rely on your preparation, experience and physical condition for survival. The type of easy hiking from shelter to shelter as offered today even in Greenland is inconceivable in Spitsbergen since the infrastructure does not exist. The experienced hiker who is properly equipped and inwardly prepared will not be overwhelmed by the experience of this wilderness, but enchanted by it. My experience shows, however, that many first-time visitors find it difficult to adjust to the special Arctic conditions and the lack of conveniences. Another 'disadvantage' is that this Arctic country requires appropriate equipment which can be expensive and difficult to obtain.

Today the relationship between visitors and the Norwegian administration is still generally cooperative and relies on the visitor's common sense.

From the following chapters those who visit Spitsbergen with an organized tour should be able to gain an impression in advance of what awaits them in this Arctic land. The few independent visitors may find valuable additional information for their preparation. It must be clear, however, that independent tourism outside the settlements of Spitsbergen requires sound Arctic experience and complete and excellent equipment.

CLIMATE

Sea Currents

The Gulf stream's furthest outflows reach the west coast of Spitsbergen and give it a milder climate than other areas at the same latitude. Whereas northern Greenland and the northern most islands of Canada and the USSR are generally cut off by solid ice, in summertime Spitsbergen can be reached by sea.

The east coast is influenced by a cold sea current from Siberia that creates lower temperatures on these shores. Frequent pack-ice makes eastern access difficult even during the summer. Ice fields and drift wood from the great Siberian rivers, driven by the cold current around the southern cape, meet the gulf stream which flows northwards parallel to the west coast. The western coast around Hornsund can be a pack-ice area at any time of the year and the prevailing westerlies push the ice towards the shore. The wind and warmer gulfstream waters explains why drift-ice from the east coast only rarely travels up the Isfjord (as happened in August 1988). The coast between Bellsund and Magdalenafjord is the part most likely to be accessible throughout the year, of great importance for the settlements.

Temperature changes

Freezing weather in the area of Isfjord is unusual in summer, at least during July and the first half of August. Typical temperatures in Longyearbyen at this time are between 3° and 10°C, with highs around 16°C (once as high as 20°C in the summer of 1986). When it is not windy, temperatures inland can sometimes be even higher.

In the summer of 1987, 23°C was registered at a sheltered inland place. This sort of warm spell tends to be unwelcome to hikers, but does offer unexpected opportunities for sunbathing in the midnight sun. I enjoyed this experience in the second week of July that year on top of the 1,050 metre high Nordenskjoldfjellet, viewing the magnificent Isfjord below. However you must equally be prepared for cold spells with temperatures dropping to -7°C and with snow that can remain on the ground for a day or two, especially in June or in the latter half of August. In August 1987 I experienced seven days of snow which even reached into the valley; the same occurred during two days in July that year.

During the period of the midnight sun, especially June and July when the sun remains above the horizon at midnight, temperatures only drop slightly at night. Since even on midsummer days the sun is lower in the sky at midday than in central Europe, differences in light intensity between day and night are relatively small, so when it is overcast it can be difficult or even impossible to establish the time without a watch.

The midnight sun begins in Longyearbyen in the second half of April and lasts almost to the end of August. Since Svalbard extends about 700km from north to south, differences in the length of polar day and night depend on the distance from the North Pole. The Arctic winter (the polar night in Longyearbyen lasts from October 28th until February 2nd) is not as severe as in other regions at the same latitude. Still, the average temperature from October to May is below freezing, and from December until April sharp frosts as low as -30°C are not unusual. There are also winter storms.

Climatic Statistics

The following tables will enable the reader to gain some impression of the climatic conditions. Measurements were taken at the Longyearbyen airport and published monthly in the *Svalbardposten*.

The table illustrates monthly deviations from long term averages. Though the individual values may appear to indicate only small deviations, in reality they are of considerable significance. Apart from an extended period of good weather in mid-July, the summer of 1987 was cold. A delayed snow-melt resulted in more snow remaining on the hills than usual and new snow fell on 20th August. In comparison the summer of 1988 was unusually dry (the comparatively high precipitation reading for August is almost entirely due to several days of rainfall at the very end of the month). Due to lack of water, many slopes never really turned green during the season. Even though there were no spectacularly high temperatures, it was a comparatively warm summer. Many slopes and even parts of the glaciers were free of snow much further up and the streams carried more water than usual. There were, however, no incidents of extremely high water-levels as occurred in 1985 and 1986, due to some unusually warm days which resulted in rapid melting of ice and snow in the mountains.

These examples from recent years illustrate that the seasons can be quite variable, and one has to be prepared for a wide range of climatic conditions. Considerable variations between places only a short distance from each other are in no way unusual. During the winter of 1987/88 temperatures recorded in Longyearbyen and its airport (approximately 3 miles/5km apart) showed at times a difference of more than 10°C.

Temperature and Rainfall figures from Longyearbyen Airport

		Jun	Jul	Aug	Sep	Oct	Nov	Dec	Jan	Feb	Mar	Apr	May	Jun	Jul	Aug	Year
Temperature (°C)	1957-1976	Minimum	-	-	-	-	-24.9	-31.6	-	-38.6	-43	-46.3	-39.1	-21.4	-	-	-	-
		Average	2.8	6.3	5.1	0.8	-5.2	-9.6	-12.4	-14.1	-15.3	-14.4	-10.7	-3.2	2.8	6.3	5.1	-5.8
		Maximum	-	-	16.5	-	9.9	7.5	-	5.2	5.9	6.3	-	14.3	-	-	16.5	-
	1987-1988	Minimum	-2.1	-1.3	0.0	-11.4	-19.4	-21.8	-29.8	-32.1	-35.9	-35.5	-39.1	-15.4	-2.1	-1.3	0.0	-
		Average	2.3	5.1	4.2	-1.2	-6.5	-10.2	-18.0	-16.7	-15.0	-19.9	-18.1	-2.3	2.3	5.1	4.2	-
		Maximum	7.3	12.7	14.2	4.9	7.0	4.8	-1.8	3.5	1.0	0.4	3.5	6.8	7.3	12.7	14.2	-
Rainfall (mm)	1957-1976	Average	13.1	17.0	16.1	17.0	15.0	19.0	26.0	18.0	30.0	22.0	6.0	7.1	13.1	17.0	16.1	206
	1987-1988	Monthly	7.2	17.8	21.1	17.0	21.5	22.1	5.3	29.9	9.2	17.7	12.3	3.6	7.2	17.8	21.1	-

Precipitation, cloud formation and fog

For those who want to escape rain during their holiday Spitsbergen is thoroughly attractive. The average annual rainfall in the area around Longyearbyen is approximately 200mm, which is very low. There is correspondingly little snow cover in winter, but it can be deep in some places where the wind blows it into drifts. Precipitation is more frequent on the west coast. Overall Spitsbergen enjoys a very dry, almost steppe-like climate. This is very enjoyable for walkers, but limits plant growth.

These dry conditions were apparently also prevalent as far back as the second half of the last ice-age, which would explain why the west and north coasts have been free from glaciers for a comparatively long time. Geological clues indicate relatively weak ice formation: low precipitation is a possible explanation for this. For the same reason parts of the central area — Nordenskiøldland, Bunsowland, Dicksonland, Andréeland — are predominantly ice free. But both the mountainous west coast, with its higher rainfall caused by the west wind carrying moisture over the open sea, and the east with its lower temperatures, have large expanses of ice and countless glaciers which extend right down into the sea.

Low precipitation levels do not necessarily mean sunny weather, in fact skies are frequently overcast. Rain and snowfall usually do not last long and do not amount to much. The hiker will not find himself banished to his tent for days or forced to wear rain gear too often.

Fog can develop frequently and very suddenly, especially in the mountains. It can become a real danger if you cannot erect an emergency bivouac or if you have lost your bearings and are unfamiliar with the territory.

Once as we were trying to cross a 900m mountain crest we were caught in very thick fog, and at the same time temperatures dropped to minus 8°C and a severe snowstorm began. Under those conditions an emergency bivouac seemed just as risky as a blind continuation of our hike or a retreat along the precipitous path that was beginning to freeze over. With the help of a compass our small group fortunately succeeded in getting down into the valley along another route which I was familiar with from a previous tour.

Even though it should be possible for experienced walkers, equipped with maps and compass, to tour around Spitsbergen, these aids do not replace the necessity for sound local knowledge. This is particularly true when fog sets in and it becomes apparent that maps do not contain all the necessary detailed information. In these conditions a walker is well advised not to continue but await better weather. This possibility has to be constantly kept in mind when putting together equipment and food-rations for a tour.

Since Spitsbergen's summer is short and can be very unpredictable, be prepared for different snow conditions from one year to the next. In August a narrow 400m high pass might, for instance, still be buried under frozen snow, be thawed clear, or already covered again by a thin layer of fresh snow.

I should like to clarify the effect this can have by using the example of the Longyear glacier. At the end of June 1987 traversing on foot with heavy packs it took about a day and a half because of deep fresh snow. A few weeks later the glacier was free of snow, the crevasses were clearly visible, and approximately the same route could be covered in 2½ hours. Any tour-planning in this type of changing conditions is subject to considerable uncertainty. Particularly unpleasant for hikers is a thin layer of fresh snow camouflaging muddy areas, a problem especially on moraines and river beds.

Wind

Like the weather in general in Spitsbergen, the wind is very variable both in strength and direction. Though sudden storms can blow up, wind is of secondary significance to the hiker but it is a serious problem for sailors. It makes the length of a boat trip difficult to calculate and crossing the fjords, even in a motor boat, becomes a serious risk when winds gather suddenly or reverse direction.

Prevailing winds come from the north or west, but differences in the lie of the land can cause regional variations. The cooling of the air over glaciers creates cold air currants which can be felt over great distances in the narrow fjords like the Tempelfjord.

You have to contend with severe storms in the autumn, even in the valleys, and occasionally they can occur in summertime as well. Two canoeists lost their tent in a storm in the summer of 1986, but they were lucky since their canoe served as a makeshift emergency tent. Even those who just plan to set up their tent on the camp ground in Longyearbyen would be well advised to use a high-grade, wind-stable model. The camp site, which is situated at the mouth of the Adventfjord in the Isfjord, is completely unsheltered from the wind in three directions.

Coping with the climate

The summer temperatures, relatively mild for Arctic regions, should not lead to false conclusions about proper clothing: for one thing, Spitsbergen is almost always windy. Wind means loss of heat, since the layer of warm air on the body's surface is quickly cooled. In addition, the hiker rarely gets the chance to stay in a well heated room. With little opportunity to get warm you must be careful not to get cold when resting.

Apart from somewhat warmer clothing than might be worn under similar conditions at home, and a good wind-breaking layer of clothing, attention must also be paid to making certain that clothes remain dry. In damp cold weather it is sometimes best to allow wet clothing to dry next to the body, or, if necessary, in your sleeping bag.

A helpful measure against cold feet in camp, as long as you still feel warm from walking, is to wash them in cold water as soon as you reach your destination and then leave your heavy shoes off. Other washing is also easiest at this point, the readiness to do so declines as you settle down to cooking and eating.

Protection against the cold is even more important when in a canoe. Without the right protective clothing, immersion in cold water is soon fatal.

Air Pollution

Considering Spitsbergen's northerly location and the magnificent clear views, one might expect it to be free from the worldwide problem of air pollution. This is far from the truth; as early as the 1950s atmospheric pollution had been recorded far into the polar region; at its most concentrated in the winter months at an altitude of 2000-4000m.

A research project begun in the early '80s with various monitoring locations in Spitsbergen supported by overland flights has facilitated the production of a map of the polar atmosphere which indicates the origin and seasonal concentration of sulphur dioxide. The spread of air pollution during the summer months is inhibited by a barrier created by the cold polar-air masses and the warmer air-masses above the European and Asian continents. Despite the temperature barrier, air pollution is present at a low level even in the summer. This barrier does not exist in winter. During the colder months of the year the cold air extends further south, which allows the fumes and industrial emissions originating from northern Soviet industry to spread deep into the Arctic region. During the course of the year the concentration of sulphur dioxide in the air in Ny Ålesund is 4-5 times higher in winter than in the summer and in winter considerably higher than levels in the area of Trondheim; Trondheim together with Iceland have the cleanest winter air in Europe.

It is striking how clear the air is when there is good weather. Even from the shore you can see as far as 150km in some places, which makes distances seem much shorter. Canoeists, in particular, would be well advised to study their maps, even when there is good visibility, to make certain they do not underestimate the distance to their destination. For landscape photographers the clear air makes the use of the most powerful telephoto lenses possible.

When to visit Spitsbergen

One of the commonest questions I am asked as organiser of trips to Spitsbergen concerns the best time of year for a visit. I would like to answer this question here, by discussing the pros. and cons. of each season.

When planning a trip to Spitsbergen climatic conditions must be taken into account. Looking at the tables on page 7 outlining the temperatures recorded during the summers of 1987 and 1988 it becomes obvious that the course of the seasons is by no means predictable and is subject to considerable variations. The following are therefore only rough guidelines.

The time of extremely short days or polar night lasts from late September to the middle of March. Any kind of outdoor activity is severely restricted and dependent on artificial light sources. Not ideal conditions for hikers. The last days of March and the month of April is the best time for winter tours. The hours of daylight become longer each day and from about the 20th April the sun does not set. However, as can be seen in the tables, temperatures as low as -40°C and strong winds are by no means uncommon. The low temperatures ensure that the inner fjords are still reliably frozen and can be safely crossed usually up to the end of April. Be prepared, however, for ice breakers clearing access to Pyramiden in the Isfjord. In some winters, the water remains ice free far into the fjords. The Isfjord sometimes remains clear to Kapp Thordsen or beyond. The low levels of precipitation may cause some problems for skiers in the valleys, when the little amount of snow is blown away exposing frozen, uneven surfaces. Over Easter, Longyearbyen is full of Norwegians visiting relatives; accommodation is therefore at a premium.

The worst months for tours below the glacier region and particularly in the glacier-free valleys are May and June as the snowmelt is in full flow. The ice covering fjords and streams becomes unreliable and some flooding occurs, which makes crossings a dangerous and sometimes impossible undertaking. The west coast and its larger fjords (Isfjord, Kongsfjord) become navigable for smaller coastal boats from mid-June onwards. In the narrower fjords (Billefjord, Tempelfjord, Van Mijenfjord, the latter sections of Van Keulenfjord, Hornsund) and the Forlandsund it is possible to find ice as late as July. This is particularly true on the east coast. Even in the depth of winter the fjords' ice-cover is not necessarily complete (due to currants, shoals, springs, natural gas-sources, tidal effects), which can be dangerous particularly for snowmobiles. Two very experienced locals driving motor sledges were killed in the winter of 1989 when they fell through the fjord ice in Tempelfjord.

Spring, from about late April to June, is the most dangerous time when the ice cover begins to disintegrate (one man and his huskies died in June 1987 near Sveagruva). At this time the terrain consists of thawed areas interrupted by slopes and stream valleys covered with soft snow. Progress is slow and tiresome, with or without skis, as the surface conditions keep changing. One of the biggest problems of the snow melt from May to late June, sometimes even into July, is the wild melt-water streams which torrent over and under disintegrating winter ice. Sometimes they fill the valley bottoms completely and no ford can be found for a crossing; especially difficult for visitors without expert knowledge of the terrain.

The period from about the end of April to the middle of June, however, provides excellent conditions for extended glacier-tours. Extremely low temperatures are unlikely, whilst the ice-melt has not yet set in and most of the solidly-frozen crevasses are still safely filled with drift-snow. This kind of tour nevertheless not only requires first rate equipment, but a great deal of experience and a sound knowledge of the appropriate safety procedures (e.g. safety ropes). One should not be led into thinking that all crevasses are covered by snow. In spring 1988 a motor-sledge driver fell into a crevasse on the Kongsbreen and, tragically, died in hospital after a spectacular rescue operation. Visitors sometimes overlook the fact that some of these tours require a helicopter for the outward and return journey as there is no other transport available in Spitsbergen at that time of year.

Most tourists and researchers visit Spitsbergen in July and August. The midnight sun remains at least until the 20th August, frosts and snowfalls are rare and the snowmelt is well advanced by the beginning of July. Access to the terrain is easier. Nature largely crams the three seasons (spring, summer and autumn) into these two months. Migratory birds arrive in May and by the beginning of July are busy hatching eggs and rearing their young. Covered by the previous year's brown leaves, plants quickly become green and flowers develop, within a few warm days, an astonishing richness and multitude of blooms which only last for a few precious weeks. Somewhat later, by about the middle of August, grasses are fully grown and in flower. Now the first migrating birds leave Spitsbergen and with the onset of the first ground frosts the leaves of the low-growing vegetation turn a yellowish brown and take on their autumnal hue.

Walkers interested in Spitsbergen's flora and bird life find July and the beginning of August most rewarding, whilst more extensive walking tours should be undertaken around the middle of August. The ground is relatively dry and the warmest days, which cause the streams to swell and the moraines to soften, have passed. As there is sufficient daylight 24 hours a day this gives additional freedom for all kinds of outdoor activity.

Connoisseurs of extensive walking tours choose the end of August to beginning of September. It becomes noticeably cooler with frequent night frosts, dusk lengthens and intensifies and you have to be prepared for snowfalls, or, even worse, rain-driven snow and storms. Nevertheless, suitably equipped walkers benefit from the increasingly solid ground as even the boggiest moraine fields harden. Streams, which in July could not have been crossed (even wearing thigh-high boots), are now just insignificant rivulets. Noisy wild geese practise their flying formations for their journey south and all around the Arctic prepares for the polar winter night.

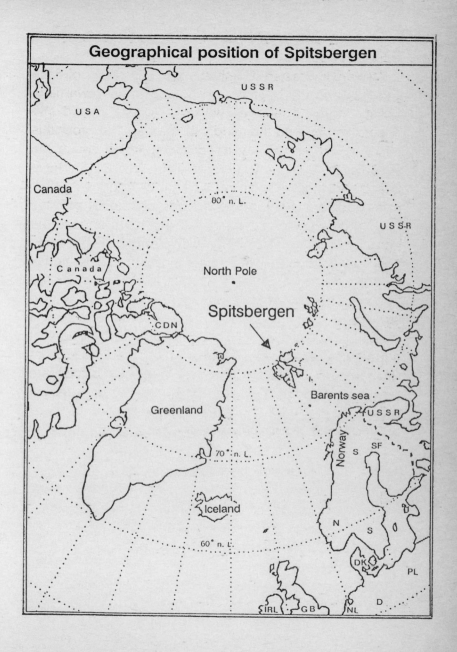

Geographical position of Spitsbergen

GEOGRAPHY

A short summary of Spitsbergen's geology

A detailed coverage of Spitsbergen's geology would go beyond the scope of this guide (see literature references). Nevertheless, a country like Spitsbergen requires the visitor to have a basic understanding of its geology as even its name is of geomorphological origin.

Due to the relatively scant ice cover and the low level of vegetation, Spitsbergen is a geological picture-book which every year continues to attract scientists.

The last milliard (or US billion) of years of the earth's history is represented, almost without a gap, in rock formations. Spitsbergen was submerged most of that time. Deposits and animal remains formed thick layers below the sea. Increasing pressure of further layers of deposits caused the formation of sedimentary rocks. At various stages the landmass rose above sea level and short periods of erosion interrupted the formation of deposits; this can clearly be seen in the stratifications.

The process of horizontal deposits in Spitsbergen was interrupted at least twice, first during the so called Caledonian mountain-fold (Siluro-Devonian) about 400-500 million years ago. During this period the older sedimentary layers underwent a severe folding process and pressure and heat resulted in the metamorphosis of the rock. During this period liquid magma (granite and others) from the earth's core formed igneous intrusions. This combination of magma and metamorphic rock is today known as *hecla hoek* and is distinct from the more recent Devonian layers, which date from about 400 million years ago.

The sedimentary layers contain numerous fossils as well as the economically important coal deposits. The plant and animal remains indicate much more favourable climatic conditions in the past than today. This can be explained by the continental-drift theory, which assumes that the earth's surface consists of various solid tectonic plates floating on the liquid earth core; the plates' positions change with the passage of millions of years. As far as we know, during the Devonian period, Spitsbergen was located south of the equator and has been drifting north ever since.

Following the Caledonian mountain-fold (during the Devonian period) this part of the earth's surface was above sea-level. The lush swamp vegetation during the Devonian and the Carboniferous period provided the necessary biomass. This was later covered by residues from the slowly eroding huge Caledonian mountain range, gradually turning the organic material below into coal which today is mined in Pyramiden (and previously on Bjørnøya [Bear Island]).

By the Permian period Spitsbergen had reached the latitude of today's Bahamas and the Persian Gulf and with progressive erosion of the Caledonian mountain range large areas were again covered by the sea. Fossilised remains of crustaceans originating in warmer coastal waters bear witness to this.

At the beginning of the Mesozoic Era, approximately 250 million years ago, Spitsbergen had reached the latitude of today's Spain and large sections were just below sea level. Fossil remains indicate that extensive areas were tidal zones. This was the age of the dinosaurs, and they found a suitable habitat in the coastal swamps of Spitsbergen. These large reptiles not only left their bones, but also footprints. A cast of one of

these, an Iguanodon, can be seen in the Svalbard
museum.

Of importance for today's landscape were the
formations of igneous intrusions. During this period
magma from the earth's core penetrated rock layers in
various locations of the eastern archipelago as well as in
the centre (Diabasodden, Fulmardalen). This occurred in
combination with tectonic faulting at this period. These
igneous rock layers are far more resistant than the
sedimentary rock below and above; due to erosion of
the mountain flanks these layers are highlighted as
irregular, vertical rock bands. Areas where these dolerite
layers occur have therefore a very distinctive landscape.

During the Tertiary period, beginning about 60 million
years ago, Spitsbergen had reached the latitude of
today's southern Norway. It consisted mainly of lowlands
with extensive swamps, which created over the millennia
deep layers of peat, later covered by more recent
sediments to become today's coal deposits. This Tertiary
coal is mined in Longyearbyen and Barentsburg, Svea
and in earlier days in Ny Ålesund. The excellent
fossilised plant remains, found in several places in the
centre of the Nordenskiøldland, originated from this
period.

The second significant disruption of the sedimentary
layers occurred during the Tertiary. Earth movements
folded all the rock layers on the east and west coasts of
Spitsbergen, causing the pre-Devonian *hecla hoek* rock
to be brought to the surface. This is the foundation of the
jagged alpine mountain range of the west coast, giving
Spitsbergen its name (literally 'pointed mountains'). The
central areas of Spitsbergen remained unaffected by this
rim-like folding in the west and east, which explains the
table mountains and the almost horizontal sedimentary

sheets. During the Tertiary period the land rose considerably and, combined with the folding process in the west, some volcanic activity occurred (Woodfjord, on the western side of Wijdefjord). The warm-water springs (up to 25°C) in the remote Bockfjord are today's reminders of these long ago volcanic eruptions.

The most significant events of the second part of the Quaternary, which for geologists begins about two million years ago, were the ice ages. It is thought that the centre of Spitsbergen consisted of a high plateau with relatively insignificant valleys. Today's extensive fjords and wide valleys were largely created by the erosion of the enormous ice age glaciers and other forms of erosion (frost, water, wind) in the warmer periods between the ice ages.

During the most intensive ice cover the whole of Spitsbergen, with possibly the exception of some isolated mountain tops, was cloaked with an impenetrable layer of solid ice. Boulders and signs of their movement, found in areas in which they did not originate, can be seen today even near mountain summits. At this time Spitsbergen and Scandinavia were joined by ice which completely filled the shallow Barents Sea; this last occurred approximately 16,000 years ago.

The precise course of the various ice ages and the exact extent and thickness of the ice cover are largely unknown. It does seem pretty certain, however, that parts of the west and north coast of Spitsbergen have been free from glaciers for at least 40,000 years.

The enormous pressure of ice sheets up to 1000m thick caused Spitsbergen to sink somewhat during the ice ages. This meant that following the thawing of the glaciers some of the lower land was flooded. Simultaneously, those parts which were freed of the heavy ice burden rose slowly again over the millenniums; the results of this process can be seen today as old shorelines in the terrain, partly far behind and above today's coast. An analysis of the oldest of these shorelines showed remains of organic life forms dating back 40,000 years.

To the east of Spitsbergen the shorelines indicate a more rapid and extensive rise of the land during the last 10,000 years, up to 130m on the King Karls Islands, though there was also more severe subsidence. This was no doubt due to thicker ice cover as well as a more prolonged period of glacier cover in comparison with the west coast.

This rising of the landmass explains the presence of shells, driftwood and whalebones high above today's shorelines. They could not have been brought there by man. Some particular shells indicate a warmer period than today's climate, following the last ice age, when Spitsbergen was less covered by ice some thousand years ago than it is today.

Today's Arctic conditions ensure that these witnesses of earth's most recent history remained in good condition for a remarkably long time. Since the last ice age there has been constant climatic change and periods of growth and retreat of glaciers.

The last period of significant glacial surges in Spitsbergen occurred in the latter part of the last century. Since then the majority of glaciers are retreating, for example Paulabreen (Van Mijenfjord) and Nathorstbreen (Van Keulenfjord) both by approximately 15km. However, there are some exceptions: in 1936/37 a significant surge of the Negribreen was recorded: in one year its 15km wide front moved 12km into the Storfjord, now it is eroding quite significantly. A surge is currently taking place at Bakaninbreen above the end of Van Mijenfjord.

Glacial movements can still significantly alter the landscape. The following three maps serve to illustrate this point. They show the same section over a period of 50 years, the first two based on aerial photographs by the Norsk Polarinstitutt (1936/38), map D9 1-100000 (1970) and the third on my own observations (1988).

Drawing 1 shows conditions in 1938. Glacier M has retreated considerably leaving moraine banks on the eastern side of the valley indicating a previous surge. Glacier E and the adjoining glacier S seem to have advanced in recent years. Large areas of the southern valley-floor are covered by their ice.

Some 30 years later the same area has changed significantly. Glaciers S and E have thawed, leaving boggy moraine fields, whilst glacier M has grown. This glacier's ice ridge now blocks the valley to the north, causing the melting ice from the three glaciers to form a new lake (see drawing 2).

Only 18 years later and the area has undergone further significant changes. Glacier M is no longer advancing and glaciers S and E have melted further. The lake's outflow has changed as well. The water no longer heads north towards the Isfjord (west coast), but is discharged through an enormous ice tunnel below glacier E towards the south (east coast). The water utilises a ravine, which may already have been uncovered before glacier E surged. It is possible that the rising waters of the lake caused the ice from glacier E in the valley floor to float before the water could utilise its old bed underneath the glacier. This resulted in a rapid drop in the lake's water level, thus breaking up large chunks of ice which had previously floated. The lake has

Rapid Changes of Landscape

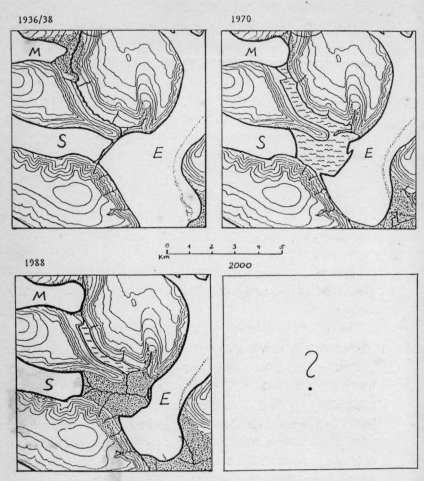

Map sketches based on aerial pictures of Norsk Polarinstitutt from 1936/38, map D9 (1:100,000) of Norsk Polarinstitutt and the author's own observations from 1988.

Key:
M, S, E: glaciers   moraines   lake

almost disappeared leaving a large area of mud. It is possible to make out the previous water levels from the old shorelines on the slopes.

This process of surging and retreating of individual glaciers has continued to change Spitsbergen's landscape since the last ice age.

In view of these quite substantial changes cartographers with their limited resources have found it impossible to keep the maps up to date. Walkers unfamiliar with the terrain, who rely on maps, have to be prepared for the odd surprise.

Special features of the terrain

Spitsbergen has some very mountainous areas, especially on the main island where peaks reach 1,717 metres above sea level. The eastern islands are lower. Glaciers have eroded the land and created steep-walled valleys.

There is no tall vegetation and above 1000 metres there are only low growing lichens. General orientation is therefore easy in these sparse surroundings as long as there is no fog. But specialized experience is still necessary to find the best route across the terrain. It takes experience to combine map information and on the spot observation to develop a practical route plan. The following passage describes some of the obstacles which might be unfamiliar to the hiker.

Glaciers and Moraines

The greatest obstacles are the glaciers, especially those that reach down into the sea and cannot be walked around. Unless the hiker has special training he should avoid large crevasse-ridden glaciers. They set geographic limits to longer treks. Making progress across a glacier can become much more difficult with the appearance of basins of slack water on the ice, rapid streams cutting into the surface of the glacier, or smooth bare ice and crevasses. These present serious and particularly energy consuming obstacles.

Special caution is imperative when parts of glaciers break off into the surrounding waters. The birth of icebergs can cause the displaced waters to unleash a considerable tidal wave, which will be mixed with pieces of broken ice next to the glacier. Boats should therefore keep a respectful distance from the edge of glaciers; it is also advisable to put any equipment on shore well above the reach of the waves. Even the hiker who does not intend to travel across glaciers should be prepared to cross smaller fields of ice and snow. Light crampons can occasionally be extremely helpful if, for example, the best route leads over a steep, hard packed snowfield.

In the area around the glaciers the hiker is almost certain to run into young moraines. Whereas the vast moraine landscapes of central Europe were left behind by Scandinavian or Alpine glaciers well over 10,000 years ago, Spitsbergen's moraines have only existed for a few decades or centuries since the glaciers still experience periods of advance and retreat.

Quite often walkers on moraines do not notice that they are walking on top of an iceberg until they reach a recent crack which opens up a view of the moraine. Basically, a young end or side moraine is part of the glacier. Debris made up of sand and clay etc. falls onto the glacier from the lateral rock walls and slopes, forming a thick layer of dirt on the ice. Other material is scraped from the ground underneath, dispersed in tunnels deep in the glacier by meltwater, or blown on to the surface becoming embedded into the ice. At the front of the glacier the surface ice melts and the dirt remains acting as insulation from the sun's heat thus slowing down any further thawing. In this way dams of ice covered by dirt remain along the sides (side moraines) and around the front (end moraines) of the glacier whilst the unprotected ice in the middle gradually melts. During warm summers even the icy cores of the moraines melt slowly and the ensuing water transforms the layer of dirt into a chaotic landscape of flowing mud, interspersed with still frozen islands or huge boulders and rapid meltwater streams. As the glaciers often have several such moraine dams, there are often vast areas of extremely difficult terrain in front of a retreating glacier. Sound experience or careful, time consuming trial and error experiments are necessary to find a way through these apocalyptic landscapes — if indeed there is a way. Moraines lose about 70% of their original volume during the melting process, until the water (ice) content reaches the same level as the surrounding permafrost. Increasingly moraines look like ordinary hills as vegetation becomes established. The so called dead ice, the moraine's core, may be very long lived. The extremely slow thawing process sometimes creates cavities, which sooner or later collapse. In Spitsbergen one occasionally finds depressions or crevasses in the moraines created by the collapse of one of these dead-ice hollows. Some pre-historic mammoths may have fallen into one of the larger dead ice hollows in places like Siberia. Buried in the ice and well preserved by the frozen ground, they have remained there until uncovered thousands of years later.

Moraines are of particular interest to amateur fossil hunters as there are many recently broken rocks to be searched through. Not every part of a moraine is equally rewarding as it depends on the origin of the rock material. A guide will know the most interesting areas.

Permafrost

Almost everywhere the subsoil is frozen to a depth of up to 400m. Only the topmost layers thaw in the summer and permit plant growth. An interesting phenomenon is the honeycomb patterning on the ground occurring where alternate thaw and frost causes localized movement separating large stones from smaller material. Also worth mentioning are old mining tunnels which close up with ice as soon as draining and ventilation cease.

In summer when the topsoil thaws, but the water is unable to drain, the ground becomes boggy above the permafrost. Some of the larger stones hidden in the morass are forced to the surface by the formation of ice in winter with the result that in summer a thin cover of stones camouflages the tricky spots. It takes some practice to be able to detect this type of obstacle.

Swamps or moorland composed of organic material are usually not very deep (up to 60cm) since vegetative growth on Spitsbergen is very slow. But the areas of humpy peat bog, formed of polar willows and mosses, which one must cross occasionally can be exhausting.

Frost Erosion

Frequent freezing and thawing are the reasons for the rather poor condition of many cliffs. Beware of places which look easy to climb. They are often impossible to cross because they have been so split by intensive frost damage and surface thaw that they do not offer any reliable footing. This is especially a problem in areas with sedimentary rocks.

The best climbing cliffs of granite and gneiss (and remnants of volcanos and warm springs) are found in the northwest and northeast. These areas, however, are very remote.

The severe erosion caused by frost does have some advantages: provided the current is not too strong, walkers can follow gradually descending stream beds which are usually free of waterfalls. Piles of scree under the rock walls offer access to otherwise impossible cliffs.

Pingos

Unknown in non-Arctic areas are the *pingos*: dome shaped hills in the river valleys formed when water under pressure rises through the permafrost and freezes just under the surface forcing the topsoll into mounds.

Rivers and Streams

Rivers and streams are mostly seasonal. Flowing water usually occurs for only two to six months during summer, the rest of the year they are frozen solid or dried up. It is therefore difficult to determine 'normal' water levels. During the Arctic spring and summer (May to August) you have to be prepared for very high water levels in the larger valleys (Sassendalen, Reindalen, Adventdalen, Agardhdalen, Kjellstromdalen, Colesdalen, Dunderdalen, etc.) and in the streams from the larger inland glaciers. The amount of water carried depends on the state of the snow-melt and on recent daily temperatures.

Most problems are caused by a rapid rise in temperature at the time of the first extensive snow-melt (usually May). Quiet rivulets turn into torrents, and surging water rises above the winter ice, attacking it from above and below until it cracks.

Even at the end of July very warm days can result in flooding, particularly if the snow-melt in May and June has been delayed. In some years the larger valleys turn into raging rivers, and in the smaller valleys where glacial streams have dug their bed into the valley floor the narrow channels carry the water with such force, often pushing along large boulders, that any kind of crossing would be impossible. Under such circumstances long detours round the glacier are often necessary.

This kind of severe flooding is, however, not common. Nevertheless any walker visiting Spitsbergen from May to the end of August should be prepared to cross waterways where the water level is thigh-high. Even if the water itself isn't very deep the strong currants generally result in a degree of soaking. Large loose stones, carried by the freezing glacial water, make it foolhardy to cross these streams barefoot. (See also *equipment* from page 157)

Much trouble can be avoided (effort, wet clothes, lost equipment) by choosing a suitable crossing point. This does require a considerable amount of experience which is not quickly acquired. It pays to watch your guide carefully.

Only a few kilometres of the larger rivers are navigable in flat-bottomed boats (canoes, kayaks); and only downstream since the current is too strong. Spitsbergen is not well suited to river trips, there is either too much or too little water. Even the opportunity to navigate smaller streams in springtime is not guaranteed. In the Summer of 1987 I was frustrated in my attempts by a stream that romped in its gorge still covered by ice two metres thick despite the surrounding countryside being snow free.

The fjord shallows composed of alluvial material stretch out from the river mouths, where, depending on the tide, the paddler can run aground as far as 100 metres offshore.

Frost erosion creates a sculpture out of sedimentary rock

FLORA AND FAUNA

Flora

Despite Spitsbergen's Arctic latitude the flora is amazingly varied due to the warming influence of the gulf stream. Apart from the typical tundra vegetation of lichens and mosses there are fungi, seven species of ferns and 164 flowering plants. The flora is comparable to mountain areas in Scandinavia or northern Siberia. According to the standard book (Olaf I. Ronning: *Svalbard's Flora* in Norwegian), almost half of the flowering plants are either unknown or extremely rare in Scandinavia, making Spitsbergen a botanist's paradise.

Almost 60% of the area is covered in ice or permanent snow. But even in these conditions specialised red-brown algae survive in some areas, colouring the snow a dirty red. Another 25-30% of the land is sparsely vegetated: mountain ridges, scree slopes, etc. However, the stony areas fascinate botanists and photographers with their colourful lichens ranging from dull grey to brilliant orange and an almost phosphorescent greenish-yellow.

Plant growth is restricted both by the extreme cold and a lack of available water to the root systems.

In an area of such low precipitation plant life would be much scarcer in warmer climates. Here, though, the cool air reduces evaporation and enables better use of the available water. The permafrost, although preventing root penetration, protects the water resource in the soil and as the ground thaws during summer a constant water supply is provided for plant growth. On flat land the frozen layer prevents drainage and the consequent loss of nutrients. Paradoxically it is the cold that allows dense vegetation to flourish in spite of the dry climate.

The remaining larger valleys and coastal plains, which constitute roughly 10% of the land, is tundra. Only the flowering stems of some grass species reach a height of approximately 30cm in late summer. Many areas are covered by dense low growing woody plants, the dominant polar willow (*Salix polaris*) and the occasional polar birch (*Betula nana*). Growth is mainly horizontal and apart from sheltered spots the dwarf trees rarely reach a height of more than 15cm.

The polar willow covers large areas and its summertime green foliage and later autumnal brownish yellow is the dominant colour of many a valley. Boggy patches between tufts of willow offer excellent conditions to wet-loving plants but are a hazard to the walker trying to keep his feet dry.

A number of different ecosystems are characterised by the most dominant species present. Moss-tundra is an area of dense moss growth and grasses — a favoured grazing area for reindeer. In flat well-drained lowlands, snow covered in winter, the tiny flowers of the purple saxifrage form dense mats of colour in the summer. In drier stony areas mountain avens (*Dryas octopetala*) will be found and in more sheltered places the bell heather (*Erica cinerea*) is widespread.

Mosses, grasses and sedges prefer the wetlands. Late in August the fluffy white seed heads of the cotton grass (*Eriophurum sp.*) are sprinkled across the terrain indicating the edges of boggy patches. The Alpine hair-grass (*Deschampsia alpina*) forms single tufts in the very wettest sites which are snow covered in winter and flooded in summer. Under the cliffs of nesting birds are the most fertile areas forming brilliant green patches of vegetation nourished by the profuse guano supply.

The period of active growth is very short; flowering and seed production have to be crammed into a precious few weeks. Plants develop very rapidly and little time passes between the formation of the first buds to full flowering. Plants have developed various ways of adapting to Arctic conditions. Many of the angiosperms do not rely solely on seed production but also reproduce vegetatively by runners and suckers. Work done in Ny Ålesund, where the most northerly greenhouse for research purposes is located, indicates that some of Spitsbergen's plants respond to changes of infra-red in sunlight. Infra-red sunlight increases in August, particularly during the night, when the sun is lower on the horizon. Plants have adapted their growth cycle and some stop further growth even before the midnight sun comes to an end. This process distinguishes Spitsbergen's flora from that of Lapland, where growth depends on daylight length.

Fauna
Mammals
There are very few mammal species on Spitsbergen. Only the reindeer and Arctic fox are entirely terrestrial. The rest depend, at least in part, on the sea. These include the walrus, bearded seal, ringed seal and less common harp seal, the polar bear, as well as several whale species.

The ptarmigan is the only bird to spend the winter in Svalbard

Arctic hare, Musk ox

Attempts to introduce the Arctic hare failed, as did an experiment with musk-ox from Greenland. First released in 1929 these animals initially reproduced well in the Nordenskiøldland. In the '70s their numbers started to decrease and by 1986 the last musk-ox died. Apart from some severe winters, one reason for their demise may have been the increasing competition for food with the growing number of reindeer.

Reindeer

Of the mammals, the reindeer is the easiest to see. Those on Spitsbergen are a distinct sub-species which may have become isolated at the end of the last ice age. The Svalbard reindeer has shorter legs and is plumper than northern European stocks. Genetic analysis suggests a closer relationship to the American caribou than to the Eurasian reindeer.

Reindeer hunting was outlawed in 1925 and today there are approximately 12,000 reindeer in Spitsbergen, of which about 4,000 are found in Nordenskiøldland. Its extensive ice-free valleys and relatively dense vegetation provides the largest habitat suitable for reindeer on the archipelago. Unlike the large herds common in Lapland or North America, Spitsbergen's reindeer prefer to roam singly or in small groups. The largest herd I have encountered so far numbered 17 animals. One reason for this may be the sparser vegetation.

It appears that after decades of protection, numbers are restricted today by food availability. One sign of this is the numerous dead reindeer found in summer, apparently dying of weakness and starvation. This is particularly the case after long, severe winters like the one of 1987/88 when there were heavy snowfalls. Even worse for the reindeer are periods of intermittent thawing followed by frosts, which harden the snow cover and obliterate the vegetation. Uncovering food becomes increasingly difficult and the animals suffer debilitating cuts to their jaws and lips. Additionally the summer of 1987 was short and there was a late snow melt followed by very early new snowfalls in August. Many animals were unable to build up sufficient fat deposits to see them through the winter. Normally 30-40% of their body weight is lost over the winter period hence the importance of a long summer period to build up reserves.

The reindeer are completely wild, unlike the Lapland stock. In recent years they have been the subject of Norwegian research projects. A long-term project was begun in 1978 when reindeer were reintroduced to near Ny Ålesund. Scientists wished to analyse the changes in vegetation brought about by grazing reindeer. Several areas have been fenced in (similar fenced-in areas can be found in Nordenskiøldland) to serve as controls. As part of another research project, controlled shooting permits for reindeer have been granted to residents. One of the aims Is to find out how long it takes reindeer to return to their optimal numbers following a reduction in stock.

If you should consider taking home a typical souvenir from Spitsbergen there are always antlers lying around. Make sure, however, that they are well wrapped — they can cause great damage to other people's luggage!

Arctic fox and rabies

The next land mammal that you are most likely to see is the Arctic fox. The common winter form has a white pelt and there is a less common 'blue fox' with a dark grey winter coat. The few remaining trappers catch the foxes for their pelt. The traps consist of a simple wooden grate, held down by heavy stones. A small wooden stick with bait holds up the grate at one end. As the fox devours the bait the wooden frame descends with some force and strikes the animal dead; unlike pellets this does not damage the pelt. Despite the trapping, their numbers do not seem to be endangered. I have even seen Arctic foxes on several occasions on the camp site in Longyearbyen in August. In 1988 three foxes visited the site for several nights, investigated the area, played about and were not too bothered by people as long as they did not approach too closely. Strangely I have never had food taken by the animals, even when the tents were left open overnight. Nevertheless, some basic precautions should be kept in mind.

There is rabies in Spitsbergen. The last rabid reindeer was shot in 1987 and since then there have been cases of rabid foxes and even a rabid seal. Do not remove the fox's last remaining inhibitions by trying to feed them. Because of rabies, the import and export of live animals is strictly prohibited (and heavily fined).

Quite apart from the trapping, winter is a hard time for foxes. Most birds have migrated and there are no rodents. Ptarmigans and the odd cadaver (maybe a dead reindeer) are the only sources of food.

The Arctic fox has been extensively researched and recorded. Fox holes are charted and investigated and individual animals tagged with small transmitters to monitor their movements.

Whales

There are only a few large whales left in Spitsbergen, due to ruthless hunting in the past. Occasionally an individual can be spotted in the seas, particularly from aboard a ship. Overall 11 whale species visit the waters around Spitsbergen during the summer. During the winter the pack-ice makes it difficult for them to surface and breathe and the animals move to more southerly waters.

The commonest species is the beluga or white whale; schools are frequently in the fjords. The white animals (the young are grey) can even occasionally be observed from the camp site in Longyearbyen.

In days gone by large numbers of the Greenland right or bowhead whale (*Balaena mysticetus*) visited Spitsbergen during the summer, but over 300 years of whaling has almost eradicated this species together with the blue whale and the northern right whale (*Eubalaena glacialis*). The only large whale likely to be seen is the fin whale (*Balaenoptera physalus*).

Seals and Walrus (Pinnipedia)

The walrus is the largest of the Pinnipedia, but due to the merciless killings over the centuries also one of the rarest. They were hunted from 1606 until 1953, when they became a protected species. These large and easily tracked animals were systematically slaughtered for their profitable blubber, oil and particularly for ivory (teeth). The once large numbers on Bear Island and on Spitsbergen's coast were almost completely wiped out, the last of the colonies on Nordaustlandet as recently as World War I. Since the animals have come under protection their numbers are slowly increasing in Kvitøya, Nordaustlandet, Tusenoyane and Moffen.

During the summer months their numbers are estimated to be around 1,000, but it is possible that a few come across during the ice-free periods from Franz Josefs Land and Nowaja Semlja to dive for shrimps, mussels and other food along the coast. The island of Moffen has been declared a specific protection zone for the walrus. It is not known where the walrus which visit Spitsbergen in the summer months spend the winter.

The largest seal species on Spitsbergen is the bearded seal. Usually single animals are most likely to be encountered during the summer in the north and east. They hunt near drift-ice for cod and animals on the seabed. Adult seals usually visit Spitsbergen during the summer months and spend the winter in the south of the Barents Sea. As they do not occur in large groups commercial hunting has never been a threat and in the last ten years or so all hunting has more or less ceased.

The commonest seal is the ringed seal (*Phoca hispida*) which remains in Spitsbergen throughout the year and can be seen in any of the coastal areas. They spend the summer preferably near drift-ice where they find the most favourable hunting conditions (cod and crustaceans underneath drifting ice sheets). In spring the females dig caves in the snow on the ice covering the fjords, where they give birth to their young. The caves offer some protection from the cold, polar bears and Arctic foxes. It is the only seal capable of keeping a breathing hole open in the fjord ice throughout the winter. They are able to climb out of the holes and rest on the ice before returning to the water.

The harp seal, hooded seal and common seal are rare summer visitors.

Even though the seals prefer to remain near drift-ice, it is not uncommon to encounter individuals along any part of the coast. They even occasionally visit the shore at the Longyearbyen camp site.

The disease which caused so many seals to die in North Sea waters during 1988 has so far not reached Spitsbergen. However there are indications that due to a lack of food (caused by overfishing) some seals have moved away from the polar regions towards the northern Norwegian waters where many of them starved to death.

Polar Bears

The last in this inventory of Spitsbergen's mammals, and the most *exciting*, is the polar bear. Polar bears have been protected since 1973 and their total population is estimated at between 20-25,000, with about 3-5,000 in Svalbard. The male is one of the largest predatory land animals, some weigh more than 700kg. Females can weigh over 500kg. They are very agile animals, despite their size. Over short distances they can achieve speeds of up to 60km/hr but over longer distances generally travel at a comfortable trot. They are tireless but not very fast swimmers, covering up to 200km. Although widespread in the northern polar regions they prefer to remain close to drift-ice where they find their main prey, seals. Nevertheless they sometimes roam into the heart of adjoining landmasses or across the pack-ice towards the north pole. There is some contact between the various polar bear populations, but the majority live fairly separately. Spitsbergen and Franz Josefs Land, together with Nowaja Semlja, form one such group, though there is some intermingling with populations from the eastern coast of Greenland. The area is defined to the south and west by the boundaries of the drift-ice, which means that Bear Island only forms part of that territory during the winter. The animals rarely cross the 82 latitude to the north.

Polar bears are generally solitary, apart from during the April breeding season, females with young, and at times of plentiful food supplies (e.g. when a stranded whale is found). This answers the question as to what to do when attacked by a group of polar bears: it doesn't happen as they don't hunt in packs.

The bear's main source of food is seals, which are at their most vulnerable when resting on shore or ice. They approach the seals from the sea and stalk them on the ice or wait by a breathing hole, thus cutting off their escape route. Once in the water seals can easily outswim the bears, whilst on land there is no contest.

Apart from seals, carcasses, and any kind of waste, even grass and seaweed provide a source of food for hungry bears, which can if necessary go without nourishment for several months. Reindeer do not appear to be part of their diet. There have been reports of bears passing grazing reindeer without either taking any notice. Hungry bears will rarely indulge in a hunt which shows little promise but costs precious energy.

Particularly important for individual polar bear populations are their breeding grounds. The females reach sexual maturity after three to four years. Following successful mating around April the tiny embryo stops growing over the summer, to resume its development in late autumn after the female has dug a cave in the snow on land. The rat-sized naked young, weighing about a pound, are born at the beginning of January. The females usually give birth to twins; a litter of three is rare. During the first few months the young rely on the mother's body warmth and milk and remain in the snow-cave. They first leave the cave at the age of about three months, around March; at this stage they have developed a fluffy pelt. At the end of March the nursing mother will have spent some four months in a cave, feeding her young without an opportunity to hunt for food; often she will have lost as much as half her bodyweight. It is therefore of prime importance for the starved mother and the weak and inexperienced young to be able to find food nearby (seals on drift-ice).

The young bears stay with their mothers for another two and a half years before they are fully independent. Mating occurs at three yearly intervals and each female raises a calculated five offspring in her life time.

Mortality during the first two years of life is high and only a few areas provide the necessary conditions for successful breeding. Bears breed mainly on the islands of the King Karls Land, the northern coast of the Nordaustlandet and occasionally on Edgeoya and Barentsoya. During the summer these islands border the drift-ice area and most years provide sufficient food.

In 1939 King Karls Land was declared a specially designated polar bear conservation area in recognition of its importance in maintaining a viable population on Spitsbergen. Since 1985 all vehicles, even boats and planes, are restricted to 500m off the island.

The polar bear has traditionally been a desirable quarry and the animal plays a significant part in the mythology of Arctic people. For Greenland's Inuit the pelts were essential for survival and their traditional hunting methods did not endanger the species. However, since the introduction of modern weapons the polar bear has in the last 400 years been systematically persecuted in the northern European seas. Until about the middle of this century professional hunters on ships, who came mainly for seals, also hunted polar bears for their valuable pelts. In the '50s the numbers of trappers increased in Spitsbergen (particularly significant was the introduction of traps where the bears activate a shooting mechanism) and more and more of the settlers went hunting as well. At the same time there was an increase in commercially organised 'safaris', where tourists paid for the privilege of shooting a bear. On average about 300 were killed in Svalbard every year, with a record death toll of 515 in 1969/70. In the late sixties it was estimated that the total number of bears in the region did not exceed 2000 animals.

In view of an annual procreation rate of, at most, 2-3%, hunting would have led to the extinction of the bears from Spitsbergen. The Soviet Union prohibited bear hunting in its area completely in 1956, whilst in 1970 Norway outlawed the traps mentioned previously, as well as hunting from vehicles. Finally in 1973 all countries bordering the Arctic agreed to ban all hunting of polar bears.

Since hunting was made illegal, their number is on the rise. This is evident in the statistics given by the crew of the radio and weather station on Hopen. There were only 62 encounters with polar bears in 1979-80, but the number rose continuously to 220 in 1986-87. Unfortunately observations are not recorded as carefully elsewhere on Spitsbergen.

Encounters with polar bears
As the population of bears grows, the number of animals which for some reason or other remain in the southern and western parts of Spitsbergen during the summer

also increases. Since there is not enough food for them there, they make long treks, covering broad stretches of territory, sometimes crossing to the other coast. For this reason it is possible to encounter a bear almost anywhere, and you must expect them to be aggressive due to hunger or fear.

Polar bears can be observed during the summer not only in the east, north and south (in these areas, encounters can almost be guaranteed during longer stays), but also along the fjords and coastlines of the west and even deep in the interior. Visits of polar bears in settlements of Spitsbergen are nothing unusual and every year, therefore, the police have to immobilize intruders who show no sign of leaving the settlement area voluntarily. It is common for these bears to break into buildings or cause trouble for sledge dogs, trying to eat the dogs' food. The immobilized bears are then flown out by helicopter and set free again at distant places. Some, however, get so accustomed to the easy sources of food in settlements that they return and then have to be shot by police.

As long as the bears do not enter within sight of the settlements, it is unlikely that their presence is detected, even if they move around quite close, because very few people go into the Arctic wilderness.

Fortunately, the vast majority of people stick to the rule never to leave the settlements unarmed and also take care to secure the camps. Therefore, in recent years in the event of a dangerous encounter it was always the bear that was killed. This may change as within the last few years some tourists can be observed who ignore these safety rules and sneak out into the wilderness without rifles and other safety equipment or carrying a rifle without having recent and sufficient shooting experience with it. These people have no chance in one of the most typical risk situations, where a bear is caught by surprise at a short distance and feels threatened, which may cause the animal to attack.

Sufficient safety equipment and reasonable behaviour can also save the life of some bears by preventing the development of a situation where the traveller has to shoot the bear. For instance, within one month two French trekking groups took the risk of camping directly on the shore of the east coast. Both were visited by a polar bear who entered the camps unnoticed due to insufficient or no alarm systems and helped itself to their food reserves, stored in an extra tent. One participant probably only survived because as he approached the food tent at night, a bear was just emerging from its entrance. Had the tourist surprised the animal a minute earlier inside the tent, this would have caused an immediate attack as the animal would feel both trapped and endangered. Seemingly, the bear thus got accustomed to this easy source of food, so next it started breaking through the door of a nearby cabin, manned by Soviet scientists. After a warning shot, ignored by the bear, the trapped scientists saw no other possibility than shooting the bear through the door which was dangerously bulging under the bear's efforts. Without having become accustomed to the French food, this bear might still have been alive.

In another case, two kayakers camped on a very narrow beach with an electric alarm installed in their kayaks just outside the tent but without tripwire alarm mines around the camp. When they heard the alarm from one of their boats, they expected a technical fault and one looked out with the signal pistol at hand — and saw a polar bear investigating the boat just five metres from the tent. He immediately fired a warning shot with the signal pistol which only drew the bear's attention to the tent. Luckily, the gun was also at hand and the bear did not attack quickly so the tourist had the few seconds to get the rifle out, aim and fire at the slowly approaching animal. At that distance there was no other option left. Luckily, the badly wounded animal did not become more aggressive but retreated and could be finally killed with a second shot.

Both these two recent incidents were clear cases of justified self-defence but both might have been avoidable by paying attention to some basic rules in addition to being a trained and properly armed shot:

* Secure the camp area with an effective alarm system at some distance from the tents.

* Never feed polar bears and avoid giving them access to food at places where this includes high risks for nearby persons (for example in tents).

* Avoid camping at places where visits of polar bears can almost be guaranteed (beaches at the east and north coast, Hornsund area), especially when you are just a small group.

The worst recent serious accident with a polar bear happened at the beginning of September 1987 when neither of the two men involved was armed despite warnings. A bear tried to disturb a rubber dinghy belonging to two scientists. One man tried to drive it away with a flaming torch, but the bear attacked him instead. The second scientist succeeded in distracting the bear from his severely wounded colleague who was able to crawl the few metres back into their hut while the bear turned its attentions to its new victim. The second scientist, now also wounded, managed to get back to the hut. The bear besieged the hut during the next three

days. Finally the two men made radio contact with a
small Dutch ship, *Plancius*, which was already on its way
to pick them up at the end of their stay. From the
Plancius a helicopter with medical help was requested,
which freed the pair and flew them to the hospital in
Longyearbyen; the bear was shot. The two scientists
were very lucky.

Not every polar bear is aggressive. The animals are
chiefly curious. Their curiosity is awakened by such
unusual objects as tents or the smell of food. Food
should be carefully wrapped and should be stored at
some distance (but still within view) of the tent. The same
applies to any kind of left-overs and refuse. Food should
be stored in such a way that any intruder approaching
will make a noise.

A bear acting out of curiosity usually approaches
slowly, moves its head to sniff here and there, and
hesitates occasionally. An attack, in contrast, happens
quickly and occupies the bear's full attention; what starts
as curiosity can turn quickly, however, to aggression. For
this reason you should keep your distance from bears,
even when they seem good natured.

Due to the risk from polar bears a large-bore gun with
sufficient ammunition in the magazine should always be
at hand when out of sight of any settlement. As
Spitsbergen is mountainous, and fjords surround many
of the settlements, the safe unarmed walking area is
limited. The gun serves as a deterrent (warning shots)
and as self defence. Thunderflashes (a type of flash-and-
bang hand grenade) can also be used as a deterrent
(see chapter on equipment). An attacking polar bear
requires quick reactions and experience in gun handling
so the gun must be kept ready at all times. Self-defence
is only justified at relatively short distance, not when the

animal is further than 30 metres away and only as a last resort after warning shots have been fired. If the animal can not be frightened off, or it is too late, you should shoot at its breast, since this is the easiest target. Do not over estimate the effect of the shot on an animal that might weigh more than 500kgs and is very fast: follow through with a second shot at the wounded animal.

Since polar bears are protected in Svalbard, every shooting must be reported and will then be investigated by the police. In 1988 the governor imposed a fine on two occasions where bears were shot not entirely in self defence. One sick bear was shot out of pity, the other was shot because it broke into a hut and was causing damage inside. Both were clearly border line cases, but it illustrates that only self defence is accepted by the authorities as a reason for shooting a bear. The animal's body belongs to the Norwegian state and no part of it can be removed. This prevents 'emergency cases' brought on by an eagerness for trophies. Protection is taken very seriously by the authorities. In 1989 three motor-sledge drivers were fined 8000.-nkr each for unnecessarily frightening a bear away from her cubs.

To avoid any possible problems in camp it is advisable to set trip wires at night connected to flares (the kind used by the army as signals). An intruding bear triggers an explosion which awakens the sleeping residents and startles the bear. These flares have to be handled with care, though they are not particularly dangerous. During a stormy night in summer 1988 my tent was almost blown away and I tripped over one of these wires less than three feet away from a flare. Apart from the initial shock I came to no harm. Only the top blows off this kind of detonator and there are no splinters or flying debris. Any observations of polar bears during your tour should be made known to the office of the Sysselmann (Governor) so that later groups can be warned. Since bears have been protected and all encounters have to be reported, the statistics show that each year 2-4 bears are shot in self-defence because they have threatened people. To date the ratio between killed or injured people and shot bears is 1:10 to the disadvantage of the bears. This is because safety is taken seriously by the majority of visitors and guides who are armed and well trained. Significantly, people were only harmed in cases when they were ill-equipped and unarmed.

Always travel with an experienced marksman, carry an appropriate gun and stay together in a group. In this way visitors can enjoy the natural beauty of Spitsbergen in safety and the bears can be protected, warned off first with flares and only as a last resort shot dead.

Birds

More than 160 species have been recorded from Svalbard. Though not as diverse as some other regions the archipelago does provide the ornithologist with several interesting birding areas. Large distances must be covered though, as only a few of the breeding grounds are easily accessible from Longyearbyen — maybe a blessing for the birds.

What brings the ornithologist to Svalbard? Of particular interest are the huge seabird colonies and the sight of rare bird species. One of the rare nesters is the little auk (*Alle alle*), the smallest of all the auks, which occur in large groups. They perform ritual formation flights, circling the rocks, accompanied by strange cacklings. The ivory gull (*Pagophila eburnea*) is easily recognised by its pure white plumage. Sabine's gull (*Larus sabini*) is a rare sight though there have been records of it breeding here. Ross's gull (*Rhodostethia rosea*) spends most of its time on the eastern boundaries of the pack-ice. Only one breeding pair has been observed in Spitsbergen. These very reclusive Arctic gulls are otherwise only known to breed in Greenland and northeastern Siberia.

According to the standard reference work on Spitsbergen's birds (H.L. Lovenskiold: *Avifauna Svalbardensis*, in English) there are 23 species which regularly breed in Spitsbergen and generally occur in most parts of the archipelago. They are the already mentioned little auk, Brunnich's guillemot (*Uria lomvia*), black guillemot (*Cepphus grylle*), puffin (*Fratercula Arctica*), snow bunting (*Plectrophenax nivalis*), red-throated diver (*Gavia stellata*), the dark phase fulmar (*Fulmarus glacialis*), long-tailed duck (*Clangula hyemalis*), eider (*Somateria mollissima*), the less common king eider (*S. spectabilis*), pink-footed goose (*Anser brachyrhynchus*), brent goose (*Branta bernicla*), barnacle goose (*B. leucopsis*), ptarmigan (Lagopus mutus), turnstone (*Arenaria interpres*), purple sandpiper (*Calidris maritima*), grey phalarope (*Phalaropus fulicarius*), Arctic skua (*Stercorarius parasiticus*), long-tailed skua (*S. longicaudus*), glaucous gull (*Larus hyperboreus*), kittiwake (*Rissa tridactyla*) and the Arctic tern (*Sterna paradisaea*). The ivory gull occurs in all parts of Spitsbergen, but only breeds regularly in the north east.

The majority are sea birds. Snow-bunting and sandpiper are commonly encountered inland. The sandpiper protects its eggs — usually about four — by sitting very still until you approach closely. Only then does the bird jump up, crying pathetically, appearing to flutter and limp away. This is intended to draw attention away from the nest. The behaviour is particularly appropriate in their defence against foxes. Walkers should show some consideration and move away from any nests.

Less frequently seen are ptarmigan, the only species which overwinters in Spitsbergen. Plover, grey phalarope and geese are fairly common. Geese become specially noticeable in late August, when their excited chattering accompanies their preparatory formation flights.

The Arctic tern, elegant and beautifully marked, covers the furthest distance of all migrating birds. Some spend at least part of our winter in the Antarctic. They are exposed to the longest period of sunshine of any animal during their lifetime, as they only experience night in spring and autumn during their migration. These birds are very aggressive, both within their group and against any possible intruders. They stubbornly defend their eggs, which they lay in shallow depressions on bare ground, by attacking anything that comes near. Every year some of them breed, or at least try to, near the lagoon in front of the camp site in Longyearbyen. However, thoughtless tourists tend to disturb them. Intrigued and amused by the defensive action of the terns, tourists try to hit the attacking birds with sticks or just spend too much time photographing. This keeps the birds away from their nests, the unprotected eggs cool rapidly, and much energy is wasted by the adults. If you have to pass, walk briskly and calmly, holding a stick above the head without hitting out wildly.

Anybody wanting to take close-up pictures of birds should take the necessary equipment e.g. telephoto lenses, tripod and appropriate film (see page 165).

Photographs can then be taken at a reasonable distance, without disturbing the wildlife.

I am distressed when I read in travel brochures for Spitsbergen statements like this one: '... depending on your preferences you can collect fossils, climb rocks and ice-slopes searching for nests of ivory gulls(!) ...'. Inconsiderate photographers can do a lot of damage in bird colonies. Their presence and noise scares the birds. Eggs and young are abandoned and then provide easy prey for hungry skuas.

It might seem surprising that Spitsbergen, high up in the Arctic, supports such huge colonies of seabirds, but the proximity of the sea provides an ample source of nourishment. It might seem surprising that Spitsbergen, high up in the Arctic, supports such huge colonies of seabirds, but the proximity of the sea provides an ample source of nourishment. Outside Svalbard, cold Arctic seawater, warmer seawater of the Gulf Stream and melted ice from the land laced with glacial material, mix and form a nutrient-rich environment for small organisms. Specialised algae abound beneath thinner drifting ice creating a unique eco-system; they form the basis of a food chain which links small crustaceans etc., fish, sea birds and seals. The drift-ice plays an important role in smoothing the rough sea's surface enabling the birds to rest and eases their search for food. The sea birds form a valuable link in the even larger Arctic life-cycle. Vegetation flourishes in the areas adjoining their colonies, which as at Bellsund, provides important grazing for geese. This very intricate food chain is easily disturbed. The over fishing in the Barents Sea caused not only large numbers of seals to move south, but also a dramatic drop in the common guillemot population; most died of starvation. The number of breeding pairs on

Bjørnøya was reduced from 1986 to 1987 by 90% (200,000 pairs); Bjørnøya is the most important breeding ground for this species in the Barents Sea.

Fish
The sea around Spitsbergen is full of fish; shrimp and mussels are harvested off the coasts but the fjords do not appear to be an especially attractive angling ground. There is no commercial fishing (even for shrimps and mussels) from Spitsbergen; however fishing vessels frequently land in Ny Ålesund and Longyearbyen to replenish provisions and to sell part of their catch.

Most of the inland waterways have such sporadic flow, ranging from none or completely frozen to surging floodwaters, that there are few fresh water fish. The river water is usually very turbid from glacial melt and unsuitable for fish and insect larvae on which they feed. The Arctic char (*Salvelinus alpinus*), sometimes called the Svalbard salmon, is occasionally found in some of the clearer streams. Not surprisingly local fishermen are reluctant to reveal their location.

Insects, spiders
Spitsbergen provides a home for some of the smaller creatures, such as flies and a small round spider, which always seems to end up inside the tent. Despite reports to the contrary there are mosquitoes in Spitsbergen but only on very calm days do they become a pest. There are not as many as in Lapland, and they are not as deft at avoiding hiker's defensive swatting movements as their Scandinavian colleagues. The relatively small

mosquito population is not only due to the harsher climate, but also the shortage of clear waters essential for breeding.

For information on national parks and reserves see page 188, *Nature Conservation*.

THE PAST AND THE PRESENT

Discovery

In contrast to other Arctic regions, Spitsbergen does not have an indigenous native population. It is not known whether there were stone age settlements similar to those on the Scandinavian mainland; discoveries at Linnevatnet are very controversial.

According to present knowledge, the Vikings were first to reach the islands and it was they who gave the archipelago its official name Svalbard (cold coast). In the Icelandic chronicles there is an entry for 1194 about a sea route to the islands from Iceland. Archaeological finds, however, do not unequivocally prove a Viking presence here.

It was not until 400 years later that Spitsbergen entered the European consciousness when it was discovered by the Dutchman Willem Barents in 1596 whilst he was looking for a northern sea-route to East Asia. The expedition did not find a way to China, but its survivors brought news about the number of whales in the waters around Spitsbergen and thus ensured the island's economic importance soon after its discovery.

The Age of Whaling (1600-ca.1720)

Hunting expeditions to Bear Island were first aimed at the extensive walrus colonies. Around 1612 English and Dutch whalers started; Danes and Norwegians joined later in 1617. Lacking whaling experience, many had to rely on Basque fishermen who had a whaling tradition in the Atlantic as their crew. A crew of 100-150 was needed to man a ship capable of hunting and processing whales.

Once the whale was sighted, men in rowing boats armed with harpoons tracked the animal; not an easy task considering the heavy seas and that the animals keep swimming and diving, only returning to the surface for short periods. Casualties were high: the ice cold sea, the whipping rope connecting boat to harpoon, blows from the whale's fluke, attempts by the injured whale to ram the boat — these were just some of the constant risks faced by the whalers in their small open boats.

The dead whales were towed ashore. Distances to the processing station used to be short, but when whaling in the fjords became more difficult as the whale population declined they had to sail further and further before they sighted the tell tale water-spout of a surfaced whale.

In the processing stations the whale was carved up, the fat boiled, reduced to blubber and put into barrels — an average Greenland right whale, about 20m in length, would produce about 100 tons. Just as useful were the approximately 700 whalebones from an animal's jaw, used in the production of corsets for Europe's elegant ladies, fans, umbrellas etc. The blubber was used as a raw material in the production of soap, fuel, grease and to weatherproof clothing (oilskins).

Access to the west coast was easier and the majority of whaling stations were to be found from Hornsund up to the northern coast. Names like Amsterdamøya, Danskøya and Egelskbukta still provide some indication as to which nations maintained their stations here during the summer. Undoubtedly the most famous of whaling stations is the Dutch Smeerenburg (literally blubber town), which was founded in 1619 on Amsterdamøya. Lost cities give rise to legends and fantastic tales, and

Smeerenburg is no exception. There is talk of up to 10,000 inhabitants, churches, brothels, bars, women and children.

In the 1980s Dutch archaeologists spent three summers on the island, excavating the settlement. Following the depletion of whale stocks, Smeerenburg ceased as a whaling station in the second half of the 18th century, after about 100 years in operation. The well preserved remains are of a settlement which even in its heyday did not consist of more than seven blubber-boilers and 16-17 houses, which accommodated several hundred men. Even compared with Spitsbergen's settlements today this is quite a large population. The excavations, as well as Danish-Norwegian work in the neighbouring Danskøya, are particulary revealing, providing a fascinating insight into the everyday living conditions of those days. The Arctic climate preserves articles well and the excavation revealed unique 17th century seamen's working clothes.

The intensive hunt for whales ensured that within a hundred years their numbers were so decimated that maintaining large hunting fleets and land bases became uneconomical. By the beginning of the 18th century whale hunting in Spitsbergen was in decline.

Barents took Spitsbergen to be part of Greenland, which is why at the beginning of the 17th century Denmark asserted its sovereignty over the new territory, since Greenland was Danish. Within a few decades of Barents' discovery the search for hunting waters and suitable landing places resulted in most of Spitsbergen's coastline being very well reconnoitred, as an astonishingly exact map from 1625 proves.

Part of this information was lost again, however, when the whaling ended, since rival hunters had no interest in making their knowledge of the region generally available.

The age of the Hunter (ca 1700-1900)

Just as the first recorded history of Spitsbergen was characterized by whalers, a period began at the end of the 17th century when it was principally seal and fur hunters who resided in Spitsbergen. This activity had already begun during the whale hunting period and even today does not belong entirely to the past. At present I know of five trappers on Spitsbergen with their own association. Since walruses, polar bears and reindeer are either fully or partially protected, this tough profession has also become economically difficult.

The first known instance of anyone overwintering on Spitsbergen was in 1630, when a British hunting group was taken unawares by ice and was unable to sail south. The main problem was in obtaining sufficient vitamins. Many lives were sacrificed before scurvy, a vitamin deficiency disease, could be combatted by the proper conservation of provisions and correct nourishment.

During the 18th century western European whalers, having practically destroyed the whale population, more or less relinquished Spitsbergen. The first recorded visit of a Russian ship dates from 1697. By the beginning of the 18th century northern Russian monasteries and some Russian traders sent expeditions to Spitsbergen. These activities were supported by the Tsar, Peter the Great, who wanted to open up Russian commerce.

These groups of Russian hunters were the first to spend the winter intentionally in Spitsbergen. Each group erected a main station and several smaller substations. At least the leader of each group was a member of a monastery or the representative of a trading house. Hunters were preferably recruited from the northern Siberian tribes, as they had experience in living under Arctic conditions and in particular the polar winter night. Apart from hunting for food they hunted for pelts (Arctic fox, blue fox, polar bear), killed reindeer, walrus, seals and collected eiderdown.

This period of Russian hunting settlements is the subject of considerable interest to Soviet archaeologists. They are particularly keen to show that even before Barents, Russians settled in Spitsbergen (thus claiming historical rights to Spitsbergen). Conclusive evidence, such as precisely dated remains, have so far not been found. Some Soviet scientists claim the first Russian arrival to be as early as the year 1000. This would mean they were in Spitsbergen before the Vikings. In 1989 two reconstructions of Russian medieval sailing ships were used to prove the feasibility of such long sea trips without serious problems.

Around 1820 the Russians turned away from Spitsbergen and focused their attention on areas further east. The last Russian monk in Spitsbergen, Starostin, died in 1826 having spent 39 winters there.

Norwegian hunters first tried to spend the winter in Spitsbergen in 1778. It was not until 1822 that they regularly overwintered on the islands. The oldest building still standing on Bear Island, the Hammerfesthuset, dates from 1823. Recently it was restored as a historical monument. Only rarely did these Norwegian hunters stay throughout the year; their main aim was to hunt walrus, seals, reindeer and collect eggs and down etc. during the summer months. Only since 1892 did the Norwegians regularly overwinter, sometimes even with their families.

Spitsbergen and polar research

Spitsbergen is a classic area of polar research with both a long tradition (since Barents in 1596) and a wide range of intentions, from practical endeavours (the search for hunting grounds and mineral exploration) to 'pure science'. They all contribute to our specific knowledge of the archipelago and to the Arctic in general.

The early explorers Barents and Hudson (1607) were followed by the German Mertens and the two Russian expeditions of 1764 and 1766. The Russians were looking at the possibility of colonisation by the Tsar's empire. Serious scientific exploration started in the 19th century with the British expeditions of Scoresby, Franklin and Sabine in 1806, 1818 and 1823 and with the joint Norwegian (Keilhau) and German (von Löwenigh) expedition to Bear Island in 1827.

From 1858 the Swedes (Nordenskiöld and Torell) dominated the exploration of the coastal areas and smaller islands. Germans were engaged on the eastern shores (Koldewey 1868, the Earl of Waldburg-Zeil with his expedition scientist Heuglin in 1870).

In 1873 the first year-long expedition was led by Nordenskiöld based at Mosselbay (on the north coast). From here he drove sledges across the Nordaustlandet and explored many of the coastal stretches.

From 1882 the geology was systematically investigated by the Swedes, De Geer and Nathorst, starting in the Isfjord area. Sir Martin Conway, author of the Spitsbergen classic *No Man's Land*, was the first person known to have traversed the main island from west to east one hundred years ago. Conway later explored Nordenskiøldland and circled the main island by ship. Even now when I follow part of his route with my small trekking groups and all my modern light-weight equipment I think of the dedication of these polar pioneers who set foot on unknown, uncharted land. The route is still a challenge and frequently groups have to abandon the crossing.

Important knowledge was learned by the joint Swedish-Russian expedition of 1898-1901 that mapped the main island along a meridian from Sorgebay in the north to Hornsund in the south. More geographical details were collected than from any previous expedition, including the discovery of the two highest peaks (Newtontoppen and Perriertoppen both 1717m in the remote northeast of the main island). Many of the areas visited by this joint expedition are often extremely difficult to reach on foot; today's scientists are simply dropped and picked up by helicopter. For the first time climatic data was collated during two consecutive years from the two bases. They also discovered that, unlike Greenland, the interior is not covered entirely in ice but separated into many individual glaciers by mountain ranges.

In these days expeditions were only possible because of the interest and support of private individuals who sponsored or even participated in the activities, the Prince of Monaco and the Earl of Waldburg-Zeil for instance. Others, like the German cartographer and publisher Petermann from Gotha, assisted with funds and by publishing the results as *Petermann's Geographische Mittheilungen* (Petermann's Geographic reports). With the widespread coverage of Arctic expeditions in papers and books the public's interest was aroused, making sponsorship much easier. Both the Prince of Monaco and the Norwegian Isachsen deserve special mention for their contribution to the exploration of the northwest. The Prince invested a lot of resources in mapping the coastal areas whilst Isachsen concentrated on the inland areas, including a crossing of the glaciers from Smeerenburg fjord to Krossfjord.

The international flavour of these scientific activities are reflected by map names. Many of the polar pioneers are immortalized on the maps of Svalbard with peaks (De Geer fjellet), valleys, glaciers (Conwaybreen), land masses (Sabineland, Nordenskiøldland), cabins (Brucebyen) etc. named after them. Bruce, a Scotsman, studied Prins-Karls-Forlandet and the Isfjord, choosing Gaelic and Scottish names for his descriptions.

Due to the west coast generally being ice free in summer, Spitsbergen was seen not only as an accessible target for research but as a base for ambitious projects heading further north. By the turn of the century the island was regularly in the news as the base for many expeditions in the race to the north pole. At this time nationalism was a dominating force and people read with extreme pride of the exploits of their countrymen. One should remember that these events around the pole were just as fascinating and emotion-stirring as the race into space became 50 years later.

From a scientific point of view, reaching the pole was, of course, of minor importance. But such is the way of man. So often in history it is the irrational aims which have caused us to expend the most energy and resources. The famous pioneers made use of the nationalistic and emotional feelings of their people to raise funds for their expeditions. Amundsen was perhaps one of the most successful. He was originally planning an assault on the Arctic but when he heard of Scott's intentions to reach the South Pole, he changed directions for the Antarctic. He succeeded and thereafter became famous enough to finance his further expeditions.

This 'fund-raising' certainly had its benefits, for the scientists had to justify their expenditure. Nowadays with research money coming anonymously from large institutions or governments the public is far less aware of what is being achieved.

The first attempts on the pole were made as far back as the end of the 18th century and in 1827 an English group led by Parry got to within 800km of the pole. The geographic north pole is just an imaginary spot in a vast desert of ice that is ever drifting around the Arctic Sea. Vast cracks in the ice appear at any time of the year so it is no wonder that sledge-driven expeditions failed so often. Unlike the south pole which is on a solid continent where scientists could take useful geological and geographical data, there is little to collect on the way to the north pole.

It was realised that attempts to reach the pole by air looked feasible and many bizarre and some tragic attempts were made after this by balloon, zeppelins and planes. In 1896 a Swede, Andrée, constructed a balloon hangar at Virgohamna (Virgin Harbour) on Danskøya. Adverse winds delayed the planned start of the balloon; Andrée took off and disappeared. It wasn't until 1930 that his body was found together with his companions on Kvitøya. His notebooks bore witness to their struggle with the elements and their last meal of polar bear which undoubtedly was insufficiently cooked and caused their death.

The next flight attempts were made by an American, Wellman, with a French-made zeppelin. His third and last attempt in 1909 failed for technical reasons and having heard that Peary and Cook had already reached the pole he gave up.

Graf Zeppelin himself also considered Spitsbergen for polar flights in 1910 but World War I interrupted his attempts. As aviation technology improved Amundsen realised the value of planes in the Arctic and planned the first transpolar flight from Alaska to Spitsbergen. Unfortunately the plane he intended to use was lost in Alaska during a trial flight. A Junkers F13, based in Spitsbergen and intended as an auxiliary for this flight, manned by the Swiss Mittelholzer and the German Neumann, was used instead for reconnaissance. They were able to prove the value of aerial photography in mapping remote areas. Fifteen years later systematic photographs of the archipelago formed the basis of today's topographic maps.

Between 1925 and 1928 the race for the north pole by air was on. Starting with Amundsen's ill fated flight with two Dornier-Whale flying boats which were forced to land 250km from their goal. One plane was irreparably damaged, the other returned with both crews. In 1926 the American Byrd succeeded in flying from Spitsbergen to the pole and back. Soon afterwards Amundsen, Ellsworth and Nobile in a zeppelin *Norge* reached the pole, landed, hoisted a flag and continued to Alaska. Wilkins, an Englishman, repeated this flight in 1928 from Alaska via Canada and Greenland to Spitsbergen.

The flights, however, ended in tragedy. General Nobile set off on his own zeppelin expedition and was lost with his crew. A huge search party was organised and Amundsen attempted to find his friend by plane. He never returned. A Soviet ice-breaker *Krassin* picked up Nobile and some of his crew but Norway was left to mourn the death of their national hero.

For Ny Ålesund, these pioneer flights were the start of its importance as a centre for polar research. Its accessibility from the sea and its extreme northerly position set it apart from any other place on earth.

Triggered by their sovereignty claims to Svalbard in 1920, the Norwegians set up a permanent research institution, *Norges Svalbard og Ishavsundersøkelser* (Norway's Svalbard and Polar Sea Research) in 1928. This was undoubtedly of far more importance for Arctic research than the spectacular flight attempts. At this time Norway was already the leading nation in polar research and by 1948 the renamed *Norsk Polarinstitutt* coordinated all future work on Svalbard from its headquarters in Oslo. Longyearbyen became the logistic station and Ny Ålesund the main research station. Recently Ny Ålesund has been enlarged and a nearby mountain is now an outpost for meteorological and climatological studies. The facilities of the Norsk Polarinstitutt in Longyearbyen are also to be enlarged.

The activities of the institute cover all fields of polar research, not only on Svalbard but also on the small volcanic island of Jan Mayen, Greenland and in the Barents Sea. Their interests even extend to the Antarctic where Norway possesses two small territories, Bouvet and Peter Island and has claims to a large sector of Antarctica. The institute has about 55 permanent employees (at least doubled in the summer season) and undertakes research in the field of terrestrial biology, geology/geomorphology, glaciology, atmospheric research, oceanography and sea-ice research.

Other Norwegian institutions doing research work here are:
— Norsk Sjokartverk (Norwegian Hydrographic Institute), since 1983 in charge of mapping Norwegian territorial waters and operating *R/V Lance* jointly with Norsk Polarinstitutt.
— Havforskningsinstitutt (Marine Research Institute). Operates three research vessels *G.O.Sars, Eldjarn* and *Michael Sars*; oceanography and marine biology.
— University of Bergen; research vessel *Hakon Mosby*; oceanography, marine and terrestrial biology, geology.
— University of Oslo; geophysics, atmospheric research, marine and terrestrial biology, geology.
— University of Trondheim; marine and terrestrial biology.
— University of Tromso; polar-light observatory in Adventdalen, geophysics, atmospheric research, oceanography, marine and terrestrial biology, geology, medicine, political science, law, history and archaeology, tradition research.
(Information source: Borges offentlige utredninger 9/1989, personal information.)

Not all the topics are studied at any one time. The projects receive logistic support from the Coast Guard's frigates and helicopters and from the Sysselmann's patrol ship *Polarsyssel*.

Further research by Norwegian firms in the fields of mineral prospecting include the ecological evaluating of industrial activity.

Apart from Norway only the Soviet Union and Poland had permanent stations on Svalbard; up to 1989 in Barentsburg and Hornsund (see chapter on settlements). Recently the Ny Ålesund station facilities have been enlarged and a nearby mountain (Zeppelinfjellet) now carries an outpost for meteorological and atmospherical studies, linked to the village by a cable car (no access for tourists!). There are also plans to enlarge the facilities of Norsk Polarinstitutt in Longyearbyen. To serve the scientific and tourist visitors during summer, a sales office of Norsk Polarinstitutt was installed in the new office building in summer of 1990. The institute has about 55 permanent employees (plus about the same number for seasonal projects, mainly in summer) and undertakes research in the field of terrestrial biology, geology/geomorphology, glaciology, atmospheric research, oceanic research and sea-ice research. The construction of a big ice-going research vessel for the institute is in planning. The British plan a terrestrial and marine research base from 1991 and to bring their research vessel *Sir James Clark Ross* into these waters.

The Japanese and Swedes have not yet finalised their plans for permanent research stations. The Swedes had planned to reopen their former station at Kinnvika on remote Nordaustlandet, built in 1958. This would certainly be of great interest as the area is quite untouched by human activity and the climate is truly Arctic, being untouched by the warming influence of the gulf stream. However it would be costly to man and as the Nordaustlandet is a nature reserve, great care would need to be taken not to upset the environment.

The rising interest in Arctic research is not just for scientific purposes but for economic and therefore political reasons. The Barents Sea is thought to be hiding vast mineral resources. Although exploratory drilling is expensive in the Arctic sea, work on Spitsbergen is relatively easy and can be extrapolated to provide clues to the sea bed. By establishing a scientific research base many countries are expecting to be included in any future treaty which will divide the Arctic into spheres of interest.

Returning from the heights of international politics to the practical scientific work on Spitsbergen — what is done there today? Here are a few examples from recent years. The Norwegians are undertaking zoological studies on reindeer, Arctic fox, polar bears, seals, walruses; even down to the detailed examination of how parasites are spread on ptarmigans. They also dominate the fields of meteorological and atmospheric research, having the advantage of a well-established infrastructure on the archipelago. Though the Soviet studies are considerable, their results are only poorly accessible in the west, mainly due to language problems and Norsk Polarinstitutt constantly is occupied with translations.

Many nations have contributed to the geological, geomorphological and glacial knowledge of the area. French and British geologists have worked for many summers mapping the still incomplete surface area. An expedition of up to 50 mainly German scientists (geographers, geologists, glaciologists, biologists, geodets) from 15 institutes will be examining the ecology and development of a small section of Liefdefjord in the summers from 1989-1991. The Japanese investigated the formation of pingos whilst the Poles have done extensive work around Hornsund and as far as the Bell Sound.

An interesting study on the course of the ice ages is being done by studying the position and structure of submarine moraines in the fjords off today's coastlines: an expensive project.

The social sciences are also studied on Svalbard; archaeologists excavated whaling stations, graves and Russian hunter settlements. A linguist studied the development of a Svalbard dialect amongst the school

children and a sociologist researched the trappers'
attitudes towards life. Other projects have dealt with
leisure time activities and the health of the inhabitants.

More practical research included a survey on tourism
in 1988-89 by the University of Oslo to provide a
statistical basis for future development.

Most projects are concerned with the future of mineral
exploitation. As coal is the main natural resource here,
examining its deposits can still provide surprises. A
Finnish firm caught the public's attention when it
announced the discovery of a deposit of about 300
million tons in Gipsdalen (eastern Isfjord) and planned to
exploit it. Meanwhile the coal field was sold to a British
firm which wants to establish a coal mine here with a
totally new concept: running it like an oil platform with
the changing crews being flown in and out. The
company wants to save the expensive maintenance of an
Arctic community which is the main cost problem for the
Norwegian company in Longyearbyen. With the low coal
prices it will be interesting to see how this project
develops. A number of studies on the local ecological
effects have been done already or are still in process.
These will be the basis for a catalogue of conditions for
these mining activities in an area that is protected as a
botanical reserve; a normal visitor may not pick a single
flower here. Yet the bulldozers are coming — just the
same situation as in Longyearbyen.

Prospecting work continues, at present in the 'central
field' in Nordenskiøldland where there are promising coal
deposits. Oil and gas exploration started in the '60s in
Van Mijenfjord and recently work is being undertaken on
the east coast, though without the discovery of economic
deposits to date. Despite this failure valuable information
on the geological structure of the Barents Sea has been

gained where huge oil reserves are expected. How they will be exploited entirely safely is unknown. It would be all too easy for a catastrophic disaster to occur which would irreparably alter the Arctic. The *Exon Valdes* catastrophe in the Williams Sound (Alaska 1989) followed by the oil train accident (Alaska 1990) should be a warning.

All in all research work covers a wide range of topics and is variously funded. Whilst some projects appear to consider cost efficiency of secondary importance, others, particularly in the field of nature conservation, continue their work through the dedication and sacrifice of their people under the most primitive conditions. There are about 500-700 scientists in Spitsbergen annually, mainly during the summer months.

Mining, the treaty of Spitsbergen, polar exploration and the first tourists

Up until the end of the 19th century, Spitsbergen was economically important only for the sale of various animal products: blubber, whalebone, ivory, furs, seal skins, eggs, eiderdown. There had been territorial quarrels during the whaling days between the different fleets and their escorts, but this was settled by the establishment of separate bases for each nationality. English whalers used Hornsund, Bellsund, Ymerbukta, Engelsbukta and Magdalenafjord; the Dutch Amsterdamøya (Smeerenburg): the Danes Danskøya. Whalers from Hamburg found shelter in the tiny harbour of Hamburgbukta south of the entrance to Magdalenafjord. Denmark made a vague claim to sovereignty over the whole of Spitsbergen as it was believed to be part of Greenland, which was Danish. Otherwise the archipelago was considered to be a no-man's land.

Once the industrialization of the last decades of the 19th century was underway, and as the steam engine came into nautical use, interest grew in Spitsbergen's raw materials, especially in bituminous coal. Deposits were exposed in many places and had been known for a long time (first mentioned in 1610), and used locally as heating material. Around the turn of the century coal mining began on a large scale; for a time other minerals (marble and phosphate) were also extracted.

In 1906 an American, Munro Longyear, successfully founded the *Arctic Coal Company* and Longyear City on the Adventfjord. Other pits were set up by Englishmen, Dutchmen and Swedes between Bellsund and Kongsfjord. A German also tried his hand at coal mining on Bear Island, but gave up after two years.

This newly awoken interest in Spitsbergen on the part of various states emphasized the need to establish clear rights of sovereignty on the archipelago to prevent possible future conflicts. Up to this point the islands had been a no-man's land where Norway, Sweden, and Russia had special historic interests and connections. The first negotiations were interrupted by World War I, but continued in 1920 at Sevres near Paris.

Russia was at this time preoccupied with the consequences of the revolution and civil war, and, in addition, was internationally isolated. Nine states agreed that Norway should have sole sovereignty over Spitsbergen including Bear Island. The islands would remain demilitarized and the signatory states would have equal rights with Norwegians under Norwegian law and could freely pursue economic activities there. The Soviet

Union and the German Reich entered this agreement
later.

Combined with the ratification of this treaty came a
clarification of the property rights in Spitsbergen. Already
established mining companies received appropriate
areas of land. Even today settlements are built on land
belonging to mining companies; the companies maintain
settlements as accommodation for their workers
(Longyearbyen and Sveagruva is owned by Store Norske
Spitsbergen Kulkompani A/S, Barentsburg and
Pyramiden by Trust Arktikugol, Ny Ålesund belongs to
the King's Bay Kull Kompani A/S). Though unaware of it,
every visitor to a town is there as a guest of the mining
company which owns that settlement, using the
company's facilities ranging from roads to snack bars.

By far the largest section went to the Norwegian crown
and is state property. In the following decades Norway
continued to purchase land, particularly from mining
companies once they ceased operations. Today
approximately 60,000 square kilometres (23,166 square
miles) are in state ownership and approximately 3,000
square kilometres (1,158 square miles) owned by mining
companies. Strictly speaking only the 250 square
kilometres (96 square miles) of the Soviet Trust
Arktikugol are not owned by Norwegians. The majority of
the privately owned lands belong to Norwegian mining
companies whose majority share holder is the Norwegian
state.

The historically determined property rights go some
way to explaining some of today's idiosyncrasies. It is
impossible in practice for individuals to purchase land in
Spitsbergen as no one is willing to sell.

One of the results is that so far Spitsbergen has been
spared unsightly holiday homes. As the majority of land

is in the hands of the state, the planning and
implementation of future development is made
significantly easier. The Norwegians therefore carry all
the burden of responsibility for preserving this unique
land. Following this short dip into local property rights,
let us return to the historical economic development.

World economic crisis saw the demise of many mining
companies. The Americans profitably sold the mine at
Longyear City to the Norwegians in 1916. The Dutch left
Barentsburg, which they had founded in 1920. Sweden
also gave up the coal field in Billefjorden and Sveagruva
in Van Mijenfjord.

The Soviet Union used this opportune moment to buy
coal works and fields from the companies willing to sell.
They acquired Barentsburg and the mine on the
Billefjord, Pyramiden. The result was that by the
beginning of the thirties only Norway and the Soviet
Union still managed coal mines in Spitsbergen. The
Norwegian settlements were Longyearbyen and Ny
Ålesund, and the Soviets maintained Barentsburg as their
main settlement as well as Pyramiden, Grumantbyen and
Colesbukta.

It was reports of polar exploration, which were
followed with as much suspense in Europe as the space
missions in our time, that brought Spitsbergen into the
consciousness of the average European. It thus gave
rise to the first wave of tourists who attempted to retrace
the steps of the first explorers, in the same way as a
tourist today books a trip to the base camps of
expeditions in the Himalayas.

Around the turn of the century, a hotel was built on the
peninsula in Adventfjord, where the airport and camp site
are located today. The peninsula is still called Hotelneset
though there is no longer a hotel. Another tourist hotel,

the most northerly in the world, was established between the world wars in Ny Ålesund.

Then, as today, land tourism played a far less significant role than cruises. Nordic cruises were already in high demand among the leisured classes even before World War I. It was a way to observe the splendours of the Arctic from the comfort of a deck chair, and to feel a little like a polar pioneer without the effort. Perhaps times have hardly changed.

World War II

After Germany's attack on Poland and the invasion of Norway in 1940, tourism was abruptly interrupted. The Norwegian and Soviet coal mines continued to operate independently, although anxiety naturally spread amongst the Norwegians about the future of their settlements. These were dependent on the mainland, and there was little readiness to cooperate with the invaders of their homeland.

The situation changed completely after the German attack on the Soviet Union. Spitsbergen now acquired strategic significance for the convoys carrying reinforcements through the Barents Sea south of the archipelago on the way to Murmansk. It was now quite possible that the battlefront might spill over onto Spitsbergen and the Norwegian government in exile in Great Britain agreed to the evacuation of the island population to Great Britain by the Royal Navy. The Russian settlers were evacuated to Archangelsk on the river Dvina in the Soviet Union. All mining facilities were rendered useless and coal stocks burnt, despite the Norwegian protests.

During the ensuing years of war there were only occasional skirmishes on Spitsbergen since neither of the wartime alliances tried to use the archipelago as a base. A small contingent of Norwegian troops in exile were stationed there to capture the German weather stations that were repeatedly set up on the islands. This meteorological information was of great value to the Germans in fighting the Murmansk convoys.

Repeated sabotage of these stations by the Norwegians caused the Germans to send a fleet to Spitsbergen led by the battleship *Tirpitz* and the battle cruiser *Scharnhorst*. Although they were hopelessly outnumbered by these forces, the Norwegians still attempted resistance. In the face of the far heavier artillery of the attacking ships, they were forced to leave the Isfjord and to retreat into the mountains, while the Germans razed the settlements. During this conflict a mine near Longyearbyen was set on fire, and continued to smoulder in the mountain well into the '60s.

Nonetheless a German occupation of the islands did not result. Even after the success of the battle in Spitsbergen neither side had full control of the archipelago since a much stronger well-equipped force would have been necessary. One of the German weather station teams remained on Nordaustland for a considerable time after the capitulation, since it was not possible to pick up the crew due to the ice conditions.

Towards the end of the war Norway found itself in a difficult situation with regards to Spitsbergen. While Soviet troops, having driven the Germans out, remained in Finnmark, Norway's northernmost province, the Soviet foreign minister, Molotov, began pressing first the government in exile in London and later the government in Oslo for a revision of the Spitsbergen treaty of 1920.

The Russians suggested that either the Soviet Union should get Bear Island because it was Russian before 1920 (not historically verifiable) or all of Svalbard should fall under Soviet-Norwegian condominium with a common defensive army. But in 1947 the Norwegian parliament voted by a large majority against a corresponding change in the treaty.

Mining after World War II

Rehabilitation of the Spitsbergen mines began after the end of the war. The settlements of Longyearbyen and Ny Ålesund and even Sveagruva which had been shut down two decades earlier were set into operation again.

As Norway's only region with coal deposits worth mining, Spitsbergen was at that time of considerable importance especially for supplying the north of Norway. Scarcity of coal had also increased its price on the world market. Production quickly surpassed pre-war levels and reached almost 500,000 metric tons per year. In 1949 Sveagruva was closed again, but was fully modernized and reopened in the 1980s. The mine has been shut again due to coal's tumbling value. Only a skeleton maintenance staff remains, waiting for better times when the mine may be reopened. The mine in Ny Ålesund caused many problems and was closed in the 1960s. Today this settlement, which is the northernmost in the world, is used only for research. In 1948 it was already clear that Longyearbyen would be the main centre of Norwegian coal mining for the foreseeable future. The mines on the slopes of the Longyear valley are exhausted, and today Mine 3 (above the airport) and

Mine 7 (10 kilometres further in the Advent valley) are
both exploited.

The reconstruction of the Russian settlements began
in 1946 and coal production started again in 1948.
Grumant, now a ghost town, was at that time the second
largest Russian mining station and during the winter of
1951/52 had even more inhabitants than Barentsburg
(1,106, including residents of Colesbukta which served
as a loading port: the two places were linked by a
narrow-gauge railway). Today the Russian mining
concern, Arktikugol, only produces coal in Barentsburg
and Pyramiden. Each of the two locations has over 1,000
inhabitants. Barentsburg, with its Soviet consulate, is the
main settlement, but the coal deposits there are so
depleted that to maintain production fields had to be
leased from the Norwegian mining company Store
Norske Spitsbergen Kulkompani (SNSK).

Soviet-Norwegian relations

Recent years have shown a fascinating change in the
relationship between Norwegians and Soviets. However
this change is so new that it is uncertain how long it will
last or how it will develop. In this chapter I describe
changes since World War II and the general situation that
has existed until a few years ago (about 1987) followed
by some of the surprising changes in more recent years.

Since World War II these relations were dominated by
the cold war, the well-known Soviet desire for secrecy,
their wish to keep apart from westerners and their
interest in improving and maintaining their rights to
Svalbard.

International politics are closely entwined with the local relationship between the Soviet and Norwegian settlements. From a strategic point of view the Soviet interest in Spitsbergen is obvious considering the concentration of the Red Fleet in the area of Murmansk, the only Soviet ocean port with relatively free access to the Atlantic.

Nonetheless, the Soviet Union has not undertaken any official attempt to alter its situation in Spitsbergen since the diplomatic offensive at the end of the last world war. Its goal appeared to be to use legal grey zones to develop prescriptive rights in the area, and in the long term to hope for a gradual dismantling of the Norwegian positions in Spitsbergen, hoping, possibly, that the financial burden which the islands represented to Norway would prove too much.

However, the relations on Spitsbergen between the Soviets and the NATO member, Norway, have always been better than elsewhere. Neither side could have tolerated open hostility in an area of such strategic importance. Perhaps their distance from the political centres as well as the awesomeness of the Arctic surroundings played their roles in smoothing conflicts.

The Norwegian Svalbard policy towards the Soviets can be divided into three parts. At first, little attention was given to the Soviets' activities or to their attempts to establish customary rights by doubting or ignoring Norwegian sovereignty.

Then the Norwegians became alarmed by Soviet expansionism and disregard for Norwegian sovereignty. A second phase of diplomatic and rhetorical protests followed but the lack of facilities for tracing and proving illegal Soviet activities, weakened the Norwegian position.

In 1977 the Soviets succeeded in preventing a full independent investigation of a helicopter crash at Hansbreen by removing the wreckage with two other helicopters flown to the scene before the arrival of the Norwegian police. Polish scientists later heard that the crash cost seven lives. The crash of a Soviet reconnaissance plane on Hopen in 1978 resulted in improved facilities for the governor. This was the beginning of the third phase of Norwegian policy in post-war Svalbard, resulting in an impressive expenditure on local resources for exerting Norwegian authority.

The Sysselmann no longer had to rely on dog sledges to control an area the size of the Republic of Ireland. By 1975 the governor's permanent staff had been increased from four to ten, with more in the summer time. Equipment was improved, first with motorized sledges and tracked vehicles and later with helicopters. Since 1979 he has had two at his disposal in Longyearbyen, the original ones replaced in 1984 by twin-engined electronically equipped Bell UH-212s. Fuel depots at several places mean that the helicopters can reach even the remotest outpost within a very short time. A reinforced steel hulled duty vessel with a helicopter pad is also at the governor's command. Seemingly, the equipment at the governor's disposal had impressed the Soviets of the Norwegian desire to exert control over the archipelago more than verbal protests in the past. The next major incident soon proved this.

In 1983 a Soviet helicopter crashed at Werenskioldbreen; the Norwegian governor equipped with two modern helicopters was able to cordon off the accident before the arrival of the Soviet rescue helicopters. This allowed the police to investigate the site despite Soviet protests. In 1984 there was a strange attempt by the Soviets to install a set of hydrophones close to the Polish settlement of Hornsund. Whilst the scientific value of this equipment remained somewhat dubious, it soon became clear that the hydrographic conditions of the location were perfect for detecting submarines in the Barents Sea and even as far as the northern coast of Norway. Interestingly, the secretly started project was abandoned once it became apparent that the Poles were unwilling to hide the Soviet 'experiment' from visitors and scientists to Hornsund. Naturally these Soviet actions resulted in considerable Norwegian mistrust. This atmosphere of local tension during the late 1960s and '70s was the background for the political thriller *Orion's Belt* by Michelet in 1977. This Norwegian novel, which was later filmed, deals with alleged Soviet secret military installations in a remote part of Svalbard that are discovered by chance by a Norwegian fishing vessel.

The Soviets also felt wrongly treated when Norway refused them the right to drill for oil at a certain place in Svalbard while other foreign but Western oil firms already operated their exploration rigs on the islands.

Later, the Soviets tried to obstruct the construction of the new all-year airport at Longyearbyen — claiming that this installation could also be used militarily and thus would be a violation of the Svalbard treaty. Norway obliged the Soviet Union by allowing the control tower to be manned both by Soviets and Norwegians. In 1975, the airport was opened by the King and ended the seasonal isolation of the islands, and of the Soviets.

The Soviets also maintain an Aeroflot office in Longyearbyen with a staff of four, even though there is only one flight connection with Murmansk every other week. Until recently the following event recurred with almost amusing repetition. In order to underline sovereignty a Norwegian naval frigate visited the archipelago regularly, as the Spitsbergen treaty only prohibits the establishment of military installations. (The Navy should not be confused with the more frequent activities of the Norwegian coastguard and their rescue helicopters.) The Soviet interpretation of the treaty, however, is that the mere presence of the military is prohibited. Every time the Navy frigate called, the Soviets formally protested to the Governor, who refuted the allegations and casually noted, for example, that all Aeroflot pilots and helicopter crew are military officers, thus implicating the permanent presence of Soviet soldiers.

As the only NATO country other than Turkey sharing a direct border with the USSR, Norway has always understood how to contain conflicts which develop out of the special strategic situation and complex legal status of Spitsbergen. This has probably been in the Soviet's interest too, as in practice the Norwegians have rarely interfered in Soviet activity: for instance there are no Norwegian police in any of the Soviet settlements. It would be hard to imagine the reverse with Spitsbergen under a Soviet flag with a treaty which allowed western countries to own mining settlements.

Because the settlements are separate contact is limited, especially in the summer. In the winter Norwegians visit the Russian area by snowmobile, often to barter goods, such as nylon stockings for ham. On the whole these private contacts are limited, not least of all because of the language difficulties, and they depend largely on Norwegian initiative as the Soviets do not own motor-sledges for private visits to Longyearbyen.

Even when the Soviets are in Longyearbyen waiting the inevitable few hours for their flight to Murmansk, they tend to stick together. The reasons for this careful reserve from a normally warm hearted people is certainly varied. It ranges from the lack of currency to uncertainty in the face of a higher standard of living in this settlement and, at least in the past, to the influence of propaganda.

On an official level both sides are careful to avoid conflict. The Norwegians rarely interfere in the internal affairs of the Soviet settlements. There are, for instance, no Norwegian police stationed there. Norway is highly cooperative in practice, since despite Norwegian sovereignty it allows the Russians to regulate their own affairs (try to imagine if the tables were turned!). An effort at being good neighbours is also made at a local level where there are official cultural and sports exchanges between locals in Longyearbyen and Soviets in Barentsburg and Pyramiden.

The description up to here largely describes the pre-Gorbochev era. Changes in recent years are on an unprecedented scale. Even Spitsbergen has been affected by *glasnost*. This can be seen in many ways. Just a few years ago visitors to Barentsburg or Pyramiden were not only discouraged but removed from the settlements. Officially arranged visits were well organised but private contact reduced to a minimum. Today one can observe the changes at first hand by visiting the settlements. From 1989 onwards I visited Barentsburg repeatedly with my trekking groups, where we were able to mix freely with the inhabitants, even if the visit was not announced in advance. The only problem was language but we overcame that surprisingly well, as both sides were interested in making contact.

Glasnost. The traffic sign in Soviet Pyramiden is first in Norwegian, then Russian.

Symbol of Soviet and Norwegian claims to Svalbard, Norwegian governor's patrol ship moored alongside two Soviet replicas of medieval ships which sailed to Spitsbergen in 1989 as proof that their Russian forebears could have discovered Spitsbergen before Willem Barents.

Also, since 1989, several of the cruise ship arrangements have included visits to Barentsburg and — less frequently — to Pyramiden. Part of the tour is through the town with a local Soviet guide. Usually the visitor will be intercepted several times by locals who want to sell souvenirs. The times of swapping are gone — today the Soviets ask for Norwegian crowns or US dollars and often charge imaginative prices well above those charged for these Soviet products in western mailorder catalogues. But seemingly some tourists are willing to accept it.

In summer 1990, the Soviets from Barentsburg and Pyramiden also got for the first time the opportunity to visit Longyearbyen regularly with a tiny Soviet ferry boat (no permission for tourist transport) without an official group visit programme. This new possibility may have brought some more personal contacts between the inhabitants of the Norwegian and Soviet settlements, but mainly they are used by some Soviets to earn money as street vendors in Longyearbyen — with even more exaggerated prices than in the Soviet settlements. Russians selling their various souvenirs (wooden dolls, wooden bowls, electric samovars, etc.) in front of Svalbardbutikken, Kafe Busen or at the pier, became a familiar sight on most days in summer 1990. Their constant and sometimes obtrusive approaches to anyone entering these buildings even began to be seen as a nuisance by some of the locals, together with some complaints by shop-keepers about losses attributed to Soviet visitors, some of whom cannot resist the temptation of Western goods. However, these negative sides still are seen by most locals as a price that has to be paid for the otherwise positive changes in Norwegian-Soviet relations on Svalbard. Whether these activities continue to be tolerated in the future remains to be seen. On the other hand, Soviet visitors also spend their newly earned Norwegian money in Longyearbyen, both for personal consumption and to send home some needed things to their families in the Soviet Union.

The Soviets have become much more respectful of Norwegian law, for example the application for a liquor licence for their new hotel, and the agreements in 1989 with the Norwegian post and telecommunications administration to install Norwegian post offices, telephones and telefax equipment in the Soviet settlements.

Other examples are the installation of Norwegian traffic signals in Barentsburg and the two Soviet children at school in Longyearbyen. There is far less secrecy, and information is passed more readily on production figures, details of accidents etc. In 1988 a western television crew were invited to enter a Soviet mine in Barentsburg for the very first time. This is indeed *glasnost*!

One of the few remaining problems is the damage to the Arctic. The surroundings of Soviet settlements and abandoned drilling sites are often in a shocking condition. Fuglefjellet, a few kilometres from Longyearbyen, is an ugly example where about 20 ruins of Soviet drilling stations have been left, quite recently, to decay, the ground around being ploughed by deep caterpillar tracks which will remain for decades. Of course there are Norwegian 'sins', but the majority from some years ago. Recent ecological awareness has imposed strict rules forcing companies to clean up a site once it has been abandoned, for instance the site at Haketangen which has been adequately cleared now it is no longer in use. Soviet standards are well behind though there are signs of improvement at Colesbukta and more recently Vassdalen. At both sites the Soviets did some massive cleaning up work — unfortunately with extended caterpillar use. Thus most of the litter is removed but at the price of a widely destroyed vegetation that will take decades or more to recover.

The Soviet cooperation has certainly reduced mistrust and soon it is hoped that relations will be just as friendly and open as between other countries and the Norwegians.

The opening of Barentsburg and Pyramiden to visitors will bring a new source of western currency at a time when the economic future of coal is in doubt. The changes of policy and economy in the Soviet Union now also affect the Soviet mining company Trust Arktikygol. Employing twice as many people in Barentsburg and Pyramiden for producing the same amount of cleaned coal as the Norwegians, the new economic strains are even bigger for the Soviets. Accordingly, Trust Arktikygol signalled clear interest in as much economic cooperation, for instance in tourism, with the Norwegians as possible.

One may speculate on a possible reduction of both Soviet and Norwegian mining activity in Svalbard at a time where the need for strategic presence has become less central. This may give way to cuts in the massive subsidies for the Svalbard engagements of both Norway and the Soviet Union.

SETTLEMENTS AND STATIONS

Colesbukta was closed down at the end of 1988, which left Svalbard with five settlements: the capital, Longyearbyen and two further tiny Norwegian settlements, Ny Ålesund and Sveagruva, as well as the two Soviet settlements Barentsburg and Pyramiden. Add to this the permanent Polish research station at Hornsund and the three permanently manned Norwegian weather and transmitting stations Isfjord Radio, Bear Island and Hopen. Every year a small number of trappers spend the winter on the northern side of the central Isfjord in central Wijdeford, Bellsund or in Mosselbay. They set fox traps near their cabins and try to live off the sale of the furs and occasional jobs — a harsh way of life.

In 1987/88 there was a large oil drilling station at Haketangen and the Soviets had an exploratory drill hole at Vassdalen (Van Mijenfjord) from 1985-1989 which reached a depth of 1,500m. Work has finished at both sites. A new minor drilling site is planned by a Scandinavian consortium at Reindalspasset in the central interior for the winter months in early 1991 — thus allowing land transportation over the frozen ground without damage to the vegetation. In the case of oil being found in attractive quantities, this will also be an argument for the road construction plans through the yet almost untouched inland wilderness. A bigger prospection drilling site is planned on the east coast at Kvalvagen.

Other smaller manned mobile rigs for coal deposit exploration are found closer to Soviet settlements. Their supply by tracked vehicles across the land has been of repeated concern to the Sysselmann as deep scars are left on the vegetation.

SNSK, the Norwegian coal company, presently maintains a drilling station on the glaciers between Svea and Reindalen examining the 'central field', a huge coal deposit in the mountains under the glaciers. Supply is by helicopter. A new drilling site is planned for Reindalen.

Apart from a few scattered huts, this is the extent of human activity in the Arctic archipelago. Most of the country is wilderness. There are no overland routes connecting the settlements, not even marked paths, apart from the winter routes for motorised sledges. These are intermittently marked by canes, but are unusable in the wetter summer months. Visitors, like the two unprepared Italians who came to Longyearbyen in 1988 and wanted to hire a car to drive to Ny Ålesund, are a constant source of amusement to the residents.

The population in 1985 was 3,480; 1,227 Norwegians, 20 other nationalities, the rest Soviets. Since 1975 the total population varied between 3,900 and 3,400, the Norwegian contingent between 1,000 and 1,400.

I would like to introduce the individual settlements in more detail.

Longyearbyen

Every visitor at least passes through the capital and cannot miss the impact on the community of the coal mining company Store Norske Spitsbergen Kulkompanie (SNSK) which built the present settlement. As far as the Norwegian government is concerned Longyearbyen is intended to be the main centre of population. Better communications and air routes are planned with Norway and living conditions are to be comparable to the mainland. Today, these aims have largely been achieved.

The Town and Inhabitants

Longyearbyen's history since its foundation in 1906 by Munro Longyear has already been roughly sketched (see *Mining, the treaty of Spitsbergen, polar exploration and the first tourists*). The town was called Longyear city and his company, *The Arctic Coal Company*, started operations in Mine 1 above today's museum from where a funicular, built in 1908, took the coal to the pier for sorting and export. Mr. Longyear sold the profitable enterprise to the Norwegians in 1916; the town was later renamed Longyearbyen, and the company the Store Norske Spitsbergen Kulkompani (SNSK).

For the interest of visitors I give an outline of the development of mining activities as remnants are still visible in the town.

In 1919 Mine 2 was opened above present day Lia and was also connected to the pier by funicular. An explosion killing 26 people in 1920 forced the closure of Mine 1 and coal production relied entirely on Mine 2 for some years. A new entrance to Mine 1 was opened further up the Longyeardalen and a funicular line completed in 1939. Most of its poles are still standing. Mine 1 was closed in 1958, Mine 2 in 1968. In connection with this mine a new part of town was built, Sverdrupbyen. By 1921 the funicular was extended by 5kms to Hotelneset where the coal is stored prior to export.

With the evacuation of the population in 1941 (570 men, 140 women and 55 children), the funicular was

made inoperable, the coal reserves on Hotelneset set
alight and mining ceased. In 1943 Longyearbyen was
partly destroyed by artillery fired from the battle cruiser
Scharnhorst and by a German landing force. However by
1946 production was resumed. Mine 2 needed a new
entrance which was built above today's Nybyen. Further
up, Mine 4 was the last to be opened in the Longyear
valley.

In 1959 the first mine to be opened outside
Longyeardalen was Mine 5 in Endalen, another side
valley of Adventdalen. Three kilometres further up
Todalen came into production with the opening of Mine
6. Both mines were connected by funicular to Hotelneset.
Meanwhile reserves in the slopes around Longyearbyen
were becoming uneconomic, Mine 1 closed in 1958,
Mine 2 in 1961, Mine 4 in 1970. Later Mine 5 (1971) and
Mine 6 (1980) were taken out of production. There are
still fairly complete remains of the wooden entrance
buildings on the slopes giving Longyearbyen the
atmosphere of a Wild West ghost town.

Today Mine 3 (opened in 1971 above the airport) and
Mine 7 in Bolterdalen (reopened in 1981 after a short
period of production before 1978), no longer use the
funicular. Huge trucks take the coal to Hotelneset. Mine
3 will maintain production until 1995 and Mine 7 into the
next century.

Through the decades Longyearbyen has been
dominated by SNSK which not only owned the land and
buildings but provided all the services for the inhabitants.
Until 1980, SNSK even used its own currency, valid only
on Spitsbergen. Over the past twenty years the
Norwegian state has gradually taken over the running of
the social services (hospital, school). Even today the
settlement is unthinkable without SNSK. One of its three

92 Introduction

subsidiaries, SSD (Svalbard Samfunnsdrift), has been in charge of running the town since 1989.

Longyearbyen has about 1,055 (1989/90) inhabitants, of whom 650 work for SNSK.

Most visitors are surprised to find a well developed town rather than the pioneer settlement they expected. It is not a rough man's world, but one of families with children. There are complete educational facilities. Approximately 200 pupils (including pre-school children) are taught by 21 teachers. The government resumed responsibility for the school in 1976; before that date the SNSK provided all the communal institutions.

A small Protestant chapel which was destroyed during the Second World War was rebuilt in 1958. About 90% of the Norwegian population belongs to the Lutheran Church of Norway. Adjacent to the church is a spacious community hall and a vicarage. The vicar is responsible for all the Norwegian settlements. He has to rely on a helicopter to visit his widely dispersed flock at any time. A helper and, since 1988, a religious instructor assist him in Longyearbyen.

The first Norwegian telegraph station was installed in 1911 on Finneset in the Grønfjord. Telephone and telex links were established in 1949 and have been continuously improved. The end of 1979 saw a step forward with the installation of satellite dishes and since 1981 long-distance direct dialling has been in use (Telefax facilities too). Following the Second World War Norwegian radio stations could be received. Television came in 1969, initially via video-cassettes sent from the mainland, but since 1984/85 directly via satellite. In 1985 Norsk Tele employed 23 people to maintain these services. There are plans to set up a private TV company enabling wider viewing choice for the inhabitants.

Considering the remote location, medical facilities are of particular importance. There is a small hospital in Longyearbyen. The eight bed hospital employs several doctors and nurses and includes a dental clinic. As well as providing routine medical services it is equipped to deal with more serious mining accidents. For this reason all doctors have to have surgical training. Serious cases are flown to the mainland. A new site for the hospital has been found north of Lompen and the new SNSK administrative building.

The town consists of 70 kilometres of roads, including those leading up to the coal mines, all of which are maintained by the SNSK. Untarred roads cannot be kept entirely free of coal dust (which means sturdy shoes are a must in wet weather) but the SNSK has done a good deal to offer the residents a high quality of life. This starts with the comfortable homes which are well-built, especially in the newer areas. Leisure and community facilities include an indoor pool, gymnasium, community house (an all purpose hall which contains a cinema and restaurant among other things), and a library. Other advantages are the canteens which provide excellent food at subsidized prices.

Modernisation in the last decade has considerably altered the face of Longyearbyen. This is particularly noticed by old Spitsbergen hands who return after several years. The village started on the mountainside on the left of the Longyear valley. Remains of old Longyearbyen, destroyed during the war, are still recognizable above the museum. But even before the war, the village began to extend on that side towards the moraine of the Longyear glacier.

In 1946 further housing was established towards the right of the valley in Nybyen (literally new settlement).

Haugen (hillock) was developed lower down and equipped with hospital and executive canteen in 1947.

The building boom only began in the last fifteen years; more than 400 new dwellings were erected in new parts of the village called Lia and latterly Blåmyra. These colourful and architecturally pleasing wooden houses provided the inhabitants of Longyearbyen with hitherto undreamed of comfort.

Recent developments also include several large constructions, such as the governor's administrative buildings (1978, extended in 1988), the new power station on the fjord (1983) which provides the entire settlement with heat and electricity, the new bank and postal buildings (1983) and Lompen (1985), the large multipurpose centre which accommodates the canteen Kafe Busen, grocery shop, library, showers and changing rooms for the miners, meeting rooms, offices etc (*Lomp* is a colloquial term for the clothes worn by the miners and *bus* is a miner).

The older buildings in Nybyen accommodate seasonal workers and the increasing numbers of paying visitors. In 1988 SNSK installed a reception and breakfast room there. Sverdrupbyen has largely been pulled down.

In 1989/90 Lia gained importance as the future centre of Longyearbyen with the construction of a new office building next to Lompen and the post office that now houses the administration of the coal company and rents office space. Furthermore a new youth club building was erected in Lia and a hospital is under construction. On the other side of Lompen, the Svalbardbutikken (general store) presently situated in Nubyen, will, in a few years, be rehoused in a planned new building. So Lia will become the modern centre of Longyearbyen with most of the important buildings concentrated here together with the majority of the population. Only in 1989 were the previous gravelled roads tarred, so dust and dirt is considerably reduced in town. Apart from a few changes in the road network of Lia during 1990, the last major building project is a new luxury hotel north (seawards) from the new hospital. Planned with a capacity of 50-60 beds and with prices starting somewhere around 1000.- nkr per night, construction work was scheduled to begin in 1990. However, the plans are delayed and it is unlikely that this hotel will be opened before 1993 — if it materialises at all.

There are noticeable efforts to improve the town's general appearance. Overland supply lines (fresh water, sewage), which used to be carried in pipes on stilts are now run as much smaller ducts nearer the ground or even under the surface (due to the permafrost, underground pipes require excellent insulation to prevent them from either disappearing in the ground by melting it or from freezing — today the necessary insulation materials are available). School children get involved in environmental projects, such as litter collection. Rubbish disposal has become a major issue in recent years and ecologically acceptable methods are continually discussed as elsewhere on the planet. As the residents rely 100% on supplies from outside the islands which have to be well packaged to avoid damage in transit, the amount of litter per person is considerable. Until recently a dump site was used for all kinds of waste, now rubbish is starting to be separated — beginning with the collection of used batteries in special containers. A facility for waste-treatment is built on the shore. Waste for disposal in the new dump site is compacted there, thus saving space. Separation of various basic materials out of the waste for transport to the mainland and recycling is planned. Run-down or derelict buildings are being renovated or pulled down if they are not in character. Old mining installations on the surrounding slopes and the supports of the funicular railway which transported coal until 1988 are left as industrial reminders. In 1990, SNSK even started with the restoration of the entrance buildings of the abandoned Mine 2 to prevent its further decay. Unfortunately, in my opinion, the efforts of making Longyearbyen nicer partly destroy the settlement's special Arctic character. For instance, the beautiful cotton grass fields in Lia were not only used as sites for new buildings but filled up between the central buildings with earth and transformed into cultivated gardens with imported plants and fertiliser. The typical and here formerly very pretty Arctic vegetation thus is destroyed in large areas and partly replaced by non-endemic and unnatural plant societies — all this in a valley that is officially protected as a plant reserve where ordinary people can be fined for picking a single flower.

Nevertheless, despite all efforts, it still looks like a mining village. Some visitors, longing for romantic and untouched wilderness, are not prepared for this up here in the Arctic and express their disappointment.

A number of social activities enhance the townspeople's life. These include a museum, dancing, sport, rifle shooting, sailing, windsurfing and sky diving clubs among others. Many residents have a weekend cabin in the countryside near Longyearbyen. There are one or two movies per week and on Saturday nights a discotheque for the young. Local news is provided by the *Svalbard Post* which comes out every Friday. It has the distinction of being the northernmost newspaper in the world and is published in Longyearbyen with the financial support of the Svalbard Council. In addition, almost every home has television, video and radio. Thanks to the 3-5 flights per week, newspapers from the mainland arrive only a few days late.

One of the most popular sports is snowmobile touring, and trips sometimes cover hundreds of kilometres, although most stay in the immediate surroundings of Longyearbyen, in Nordenskiøldland. The 1,050 inhabitants own no fewer than 900 registered 'scooters'; cars and motorcycles are much less common.

The suspicion that reindeer were being disturbed by the traffic in the countryside cannot be confirmed by scientific studies. The animals appeared to adjust quickly to the passing vehicles as long as they were not approached too closely. In general almost all snowmobile excursions stick to a few fixed routes which usually lead to private cabins, other settlements, or to one of the cabins maintained by the sporting club or the SNSK.

A large number of Longyearbyen residents spend the snow-free months in the south, either in Norway or abroad, so the city appears deserted in July and August. Many of the Norwegians you meet at this time are not permanent residents but temporary help filling in during the summer vacation.

Although salaries are about the same as those in the rest of Norway, the taxes are much lower because of the Svalbard Treaty. Additional advantages such as low rents for the SNSK's comfortable homes add to the attraction. So for every job opening there are enough applicants and the majority of workers stay on for many years, often until they retire.

Provisions for the local community are ordered mainly through the SNSK depot. Other shops supply a limited range of perishable goods. The system will change in the

near future. The enlarged Svalbard Butikken (general
store) is planned next to Lompen which will provide
everything and operate as a normal retail shop. It cannot
be taken for granted that specialist requirements of
dehydrated foods and outdoor equipment will be
available for visitors though. It will still be advisable for
expeditions to bring all they will need with them.

Coal Production and its alternatives

During the two month summer vacation the SNSK stops
coal production and repairs installations. Visitors during
this time are rarely aware of any mining activities.

Presently in operation are Pit 3 (above the airport, the
air-conditioning is audible at the camp site as a constant
low background noise) and Pit 7 (to the east of
Bolterdalen, 11km from Longyearbyen towards
Adventdalen).

Known reserves of Pit 3 are about 1,400,000 tonnes
and of Pit 7 about 3,200,000 tonnes. Continued mining
in Longyearbyen is secured well into the next century, at
least in Pit 7. Other further deposits are being
investigated. The currently favoured method of mining is
the so called *longwall* method; the coal seam is mined
on a long front between two parallel tunnels. Hydraulic
props are used at the coal face to support the cavity
roof. As the seam is driven further into the rock the large
cavities created by earlier mining activities are filled by
allowing the roofs to collapse. The pits use the latest
technology and most of the equipment comes from
Great Britain. Productivity per man (and woman, there is
one female miner) is higher than in any other European
coal mining area.

Huge lorries take coal from both pits to Hotelneset, where it is sorted and graded. Up until 1988 part of the coal was transported by funicular, but the installation has now been dismantled.

The coal is sorted into three size categories on the Hotelneset peninsula. Coal up to 6mm in diameter is mainly used in power stations and in the production of coke used in the steel industry. Norway took most of this grade. However the closure of the coke works in Mo i Rana has emphasized the need to find new customers. The second grade, from 6mm to 25mm, achieves the highest prices and is largely used in the Norwegian steel industry. The pieces over 25mm serve as household fuel, and were once used in steam boilers for locomotives and ships. In former times there was a big market for this grade in Norway for heating purposes, but it has now lost much of its importance. More than two thirds of the coal today is sold outside Norway. The annual production goal has been reduced from 500,000 to 300,000 tonnes in response to the low coal price.

From Hotelneset the coal is loaded on to freighters during the ice free period; usually mid-May to mid-December. Thanks to its high calorific value and low sulphur content (around 1%), coal from Spitsbergen is easier to market than other deposits. Mining is also relatively easy, since the approximately one metre thick stratum is situated at about 200 metres above sea level and is mainly located in the permafrost level. This means that problems of flooding in the mines are infrequent. The tunnels have to be ventilated to prevent the formation of ice from condensing water.

The Norwegian government has to subsidize the mines with a total of about 150 million nkr. per year due to the expense of maintaining such a remote mining community. According to the SNSK's records, however, the subsidy per tonne of coal is still lower than for coal mined in Western Germany.

A gradual economic diversification is the goal of Norwegian policy for Longyearbyen, creating new jobs outside the unprofitable coal-mining industry to maintain the present number of inhabitants. A few small firms without need for much transportation have been attracted already by tax advantages due to the Svalbard Treaty. Such diverse enterprises as Norway's only diamond cutter or a translator of books into braille have already been established.

With the installation of the new luxury hotel, tourism will contribute an important share to the economy, creating new jobs and bringing in wealth. As a replacement for coal mining, tourism might well turn out to be less of a problem for the Arctic environment as most of the tourist activities will be concentrated in and around Longyearbyen, such as fjord cruises and round flights, and will not interfere with the balance of nature. Only a few visitors will accept the hardships of trekking and venture further afield.

For continued coal mining new coal fields will have to be exploited. Whilst the majority of present mines are close to the sea new developments will be inland. This would mean considerable damage to the environment in as yet untouched areas. For the first time in Spitsbergen a macadamed road is planned to a new mine site and beyond to the settlement of Sveagruva. An oil exploration rig is foreseen in the same area adding further pressure for its construction. The road will not only connect two settlements for the first time but, more worrying, might attract easy hiking tours. Areas that today are only accessible to small groups of well-equipped, fit hikers will

Arctic fox.

Svalbard reindeer. When the first snows announce the coming winter the animals must be fat to survive the harsh months ahead.

Walruses are a rare sight. (Photo by V. Sandkühler)

The Svalbard poppy.

Flowering cotton grass in a sheltered, inland valley.

Children playing in Longyearbyen.

The northernmost train in the world at Ny Ålesund.

Camping by Krossfjorden. (Photo by Vic Royce)

View of Magdalenefjorden, northwest Spitsbergen. (Photo by Vic Royce)

be open to far more day tourists with the corresponding consequences for the environment. Except in the unlikelihood of the road being restricted to mining use only, its construction will therefore cut a wide belt of human activity into the Arctic that far exceeds the area that will be affected by the mining alone. Under these conditions starting coal mining in these unspoiled areas may have far reaching consequences.

Compared to this, the development of exclusive tourism with the construction of a top quality hotel is likely to have far less serious ecological consequences as that kind of exclusive tourism is likely to concentrate just on Longyearbyen, some comfortable ship excursions and sight-seeing flights. The new road, however, would not only damage the inland nature and the mine, but in addition would open up the interior for relatively mass tourism, which causes various problems without being of particular economic interest for the local communities. However, in these days of reduced east-west tension and an equally vanishing pressure on Norway to maintain a massive engagement in Svalbard to defend its sovereignty against the Soviets, it is imaginable that the Norwegian *Storting* (parliament) is not willing forever to pump vast subsidies into maintaining coal-mining on Svalbard at its present scale. A reduction of subsidies and a further increase of ecological consciousness may be the end of the present ambitious plans for the road and the new mines. On a lower level, coal mining can also be continued from Sveagruva, thus leaving the interior unspoilt.

There are rumours that the Soviets are considering a reduced coal mining programme in the future. With a Soviet economy that increasingly has to follow market principles, the Trust Arktikugol coal mining on Svalbard, using twice as many people for about the same net coal production as the Norwegian SNSK, is certainly facing difficult times. A reduction of the Soviet mining programme and attempts to build up other economic activities in the Soviet settlements on Svalbard or an elimination of Soviet activity altogether therefore would not be too surprising. This in turn would facilitate a reduced Norwegian engagement on Svalbard.

Barentsburg

Barentsburg, the main Soviet settlement, was founded in 1920 on the Grønfjord by the Dutch. Previously there was a nearby Norwegian whaling station, telegraph station on Finneset and an exploratory coal mine. Following the Wall Street Crash and the subsequent economic crisis the Dutch ceased to operate the mines and the Soviet state-owned Trust Arktikugol bought the settlement and the adjoining lands in 1932. During the evacuation in 1941 and the later destruction in 1943 by the battleship *Tirpitz*, Barentsburg, like Longyearbyen, was largely destroyed. The Soviets began to rebuild the settlement in 1948. Grumantbyen was closed down as the coal seam was exhausted, which meant that Barentsburg became their main settlement.

The Trust Arktikugol's administrative buildings as well as the newly built (1983) imposing consulate are found here. Barentsburg, like Longyearbyen, has seen extensive building works in recent years. In the last fifteen years Barentsburg's population has been somewhere between 1100 and 1450. In 1975 a new power station was added and in 1984 a large research centre was completed.

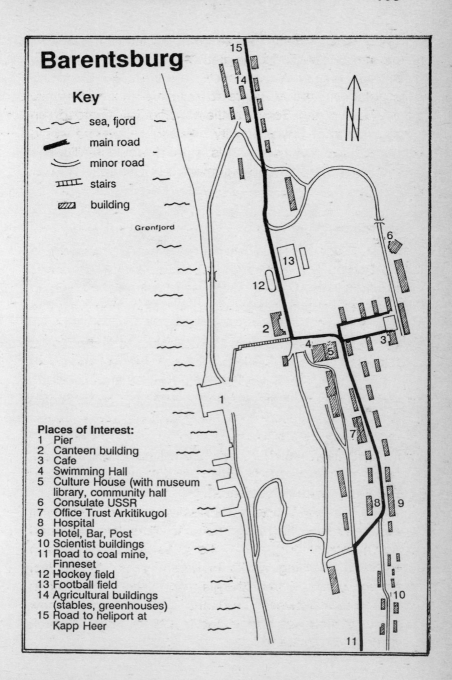

Barentsburg

Key

〜〜 ― sea, fjord
▬▬ main road
⌒⌒ minor road
ⅢⅢ stairs
▨ building

Grønfjord

15
14
13
12
2
4
5
3
6
7
8 9
1
10
11

Places of Interest:
1 Pier
2 Canteen building
3 Cafe
4 Swimming Hall
5 Culture House (with museum library, community hall
6 Consulate USSR
7 Office Trust Arkitikugol
8 Hospital
9 Hotel, Bar, Post
10 Scientist buildings
11 Road to coal mine, Finneset
12 Hockey field
13 Football field
14 Agricultural buildings (stables, greenhouses)
15 Road to heliport at Kapp Heer

The social welfare provisions in Barentsburg are extensive and impressive. Cultural activities by the inhabitants are supported and encouraged. The main centre is the culture house which offers not only a chess room but a 30,000 volume library, a 450 seat hall for showing films, theatre and shows and a museum.

The museum was opened in 1963 and covers natural history topics and has extensive coverage of Soviet activities in Spitsbergen. Most of the exhibits were prepared by residents of Barentsburg. The Soviets try to prove their presence on the islands before Barents and even before the Vikings. The expedition of Rusanov is well documented. He came to Svalbard in 1912 on board *Hercules*, did some geological surveys and placed 28 claim posts in the field, thus securing the first coal fields and land claims for Russia in an area around Grumant. Rusanov later tried to reach the north pole but disappeared in the attempt. Twenty two years later remains of his ship were found on the Siberian Taimyr peninsula. A second museum dedicated to him is at Rusanovodden near Colesbukta.

The culture house also offers an impressive range of sports facilities: in all there are 15 disciplines regularly practised supported by several trainers, a huge hall with a spectator stand, a fitness room, and a big salt-water swimming pool. The pool is open every day except Monday from 11.00-23.00 hours. The main pool is 25m in length and the water is maintained at 27°C; there is an additional children's pool. The building has been architect designed and houses many plants which give an almost tropical impression in sharp contrast to the Arctic landscape visible through the huge side window.

There is also an outdoor hockey field and the residents practise cross country skiing. Several sporting competitions are held between Barentsburg and Pyramiden each year as well as between the Norwegian settlements.

In their homes the residents can receive one Soviet television channel.

Work contracts are generally for two years; some stay an additional year. Both living conditions and salaries are higher than at home and having worked in this distant outpost they are often rewarded with better possibilities for housing on their return. Apart from these material advantages it was often one of the few chances to visit another country. About 600 of Barentsburg's inhabitants are directly engaged in mining (annual production about 350,000 tonnes), others in community or social services.

The new scientific complex is almost deserted during winter time; only the meteorological station is operated throughout the year. During the summer up to 400 Soviet researchers arrive, increasing the population then to around 1,400.

About 25% of the population are women and there are about 150 children. The Soviet mining company Trust Arktikugol maintains both a kindergarten and primary school (older children have to return to the Soviet mainland for schooling), and a hospital with 20 doctors.

A speciality of the Soviet settlements is their agricultural complex. Barentsburg has a herd of 35 cows, two bulls, hens, pigs and large greenhouses for vegetables. They are almost self sufficient, but most of the animal feed has to be imported. There are interesting attempts to use natural resources. On one of our tours in 1989 we met people drying seaweed on the old pier of abandoned Colesbukta for shipment to Barentsburg where it is fed to the cattle.

Not far to the north of the settlement (Heerodden) is the Soviet heliport, where five large Aeroflot transporter helicopters are stationed. The heliport became operational in 1960 and enlarged in the late '70s. It now comprises hangars, workshops and stores, accommodation for personnel and a large radar installation. Nearby is an observation station for the northern lights and atmospheric studies.

Just outside the border of the Trust Arktikugol's property in Barentsburg the Norwegian governor maintains a small house, garage and official car for his visits here.

All Soviet mineral explorations in the Nordenskiøldland are based in Barentsburg. They use tracked vehicles throughout the year to carry provisions over long distances, which has in the past caused some friction with the Norwegian governor. To use tracked vehicles off the road is only permitted when the ground is frozen solid; at any other time of the year the vehicles seriously damage the vegetation.

Frequently walkers encounter the untidy remains of drilling stations; an unpleasant experience. A particularly sad example is the Fuglefjellet between Longyearbyen and Colesbukta. On its high plateau (an area of approximately three square kilometres) more than 20 drilling stations are rusting away. The coal deposits of the Trust Arktikugol's claims around Barentsburg have already been exhausted and coal is mined from sites rented from the SNSK. In late 1987 negotiations concerning continued mining of SNSK deposits after the current agreement expires in 1997 were not successful. Considering the numerous new buildings in Barentsburg it does not appear to be a settlement the Soviets are keen to abandon.

As already mentioned in the chapter on Soviet-Norwegian relations, these have become much more relaxed during the last few years. Glasnost — openness — is practised by the Soviets today to an extent that was unthinkable just a few years ago. No longer is there any difficulty in visiting Barentsburg. In fact there is now an understanding that western curiosity can be a source of income and Russian souvenirs are on offer, kopeks are offered to tourists and even the Soviet pictorial book on Svalbard has been translated for sale to visitors. The canteen is open for meals at an impressive (1989) price of 90.-nkr. Guided tours are also arranged for groups with or without accommodation and meals.

Further association with the Norwegian administration includes the installation of Norwegian traffic lights, telephone system, telefax and a Norwegian post office. A 45 minute film on Svalbard, showing daily life in the settlement and the workings of a Soviet coal mine was made in 1988 by a German television crew who spent several days in Barentsburg. This was the first time that a western TV team had been invited to participate in such a venture.

Day trips by boat are offered to tourists during the summer on a stand-by basis from Longyearbyen. The dates are usually only known a few days or perhaps weeks in advance, so they can generally not be booked in advance. There are also a few international tour operators who include, among other destinations, a visit to Barentsburg by coastal vessels or as part of major trekking tours (see *Small coastal vessel trips* and *Trekking*). Another possibility is the charter of a helicopter.

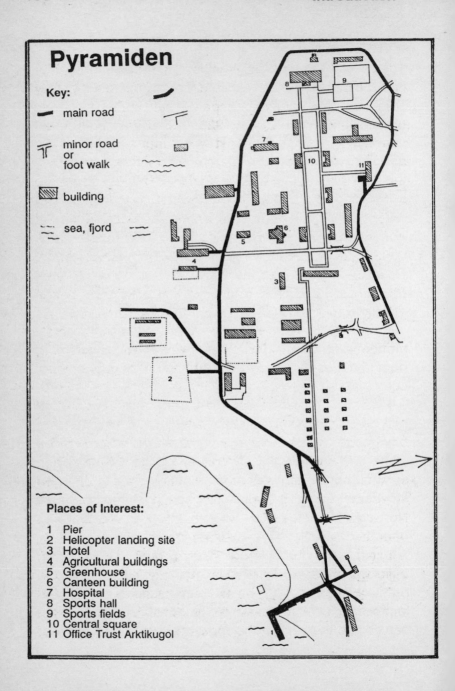

Pyramiden

Key:

— main road

⊤ minor road
or
foot walk

▨ building

≈ sea, fjord

Places of Interest:

1   Pier
2   Helicopter landing site
3   Hotel
4   Agricultural buildings
5   Greenhouse
6   Canteen building
7   Hospital
8   Sports hall
9   Sports fields
10 Central square
11 Office Trust Arktikugol

Pyramiden

The second largest Soviet settlement (population 1,000) is at the Billefjord in the northeast of the Isfjord. Originally Swedish, the mining company ran into economic difficulties and sold out in 1926 to the Russky Grumant company; in 1931 the Trust Arktikugol took over. By about 1948 coal production resumed and at some time the Soviet consulate was based here. Rich coalfields are still waiting to be exploited in this area, and coal mining will continue in Pyramiden for the foreseeable future. Annual coal production is about 250,000 tonnes and is transported to Murmansk from April to late autumn. Occasionally the Soviets have to use one of their powerful ice-breakers to open up the route from the mainland to Pyramiden through the winter fjord ice.

From 1975 to 1985 Pyramiden was extensively modernised. About 130 new flats were built, a swimming pool (the most northerly on earth) and a new agricultural complex which includes greenhouses and a dairy herd.

Pyramiden is very isolated, though less so now with a new international telephone network. In the past the officials were rather unwelcoming to casual visitors. Since 1988, however, organised cruises visiting Pyramiden in summer have been welcomed. A landing fee is charged for boats using the pier just as in Barentsburg. A Norwegian post office was installed in April 1990, operated by a Soviet as in Barentsburg.

Except for the central square and the modern buildings, Pyramiden itself is not exactly a neat and pretty place but it has a remarkable view of the impressive, heavily crevassed Nordenskiold glacier that carves into the sea on the opposite side of the Billefjord and the finely shaped Pyramid mountain rising above the village named after it.

Ny Ålesund

Ny Ålesund, the world's northernmost permanently inhabited settlement, was founded by the Kings's Bay Kull Company in 1916 as a coal mining centre. Unlike all the other coal-seams in Spitsbergen, the deposits in Ny Ålesund are near the coast and deep down below sea level, below the level of the permafrost and extremely difficult to extract. Major accidents since 1929 have caused the deaths of nearly 70 people. Despite modernization a final tragic accident in 1962 finally led to the closure of the mine and even caused a crisis for the government in Oslo.

The end of mining meant a considerable change for this settlement where in 1923 there were 388 people living, mostly working for the King's Bay Kull Company. At this time, and until the Second World War, the settlement had its own small hospital with a dentist, a library, cafe and school with up to 30 pupils, and its own newspaper until the 1941 evacuation.

Today there remain the shafts and a lovingly restored railway engine which once transported coal to the loading areas. There have been considerable efforts in recent years to restore and retain many of Ny Ålesund's historical features. Not long ago a small museum opened its doors. Amundsen's memorial and the site of the hangar of his Zeppelin *Norge* is here as a reminder of the great days of the race to the North Pole.

Ny Ålesund is used mainly as a research base. The core population during the winter is only about 12, but during the summer there are more than a hundred scientists. Permanent jobs are meteorological and seismic observations and atmospheric studies (Norsk Institutt for Luftforskning). Since 1989 the outpost on Zeppelinfjellet, accessible by funicular that leads to the top of this mountain above Ny Ålesund, is used for atmospheric studies. From 1990 onwards the German Alfred Wegener Institut will operate its own polar research station here mainly for meteorological and marine biological work throughout the year. British and Japanese institutions have also shown interest in establishing permanent bases here from 1991. French researchers have had their summer camp close to the village for a number of years and produced, among other publications, a geomorphological map of the Brøgger-peninsula (see *Bibliography*).

Over the years Ny Ålesund has changed from being a mining settlement to a scientific community. The former mining company has now become a service firm that rents out the infrastructure for the scientific work. Science is very much in evidence in Ny Ålesund and the visitor will see numerous installations around and is asked not to tamper with them. Many visitors attend conferences on Arctic topics and thousands of day tourists arrive on cruises or by small coastal boat (see *Tourism*) or by chartered helicopter. The King's Bay Kull Company charges an entry fee of 10.-nkr per head.

There is a private airstrip suitable for small planes. Many things in Ny Ålesund are 'the most northerly', amongst them the post office (open only during the summer), a small art gallery and a patch of ground which has been declared 'the most northerly camp site'. The kiosk offers a very limited range of goods to tourists and there is a souvenir shop too.

The spectacular landscape and setting of Ny Ålesund and the Kongsfjord, Krossfjord and Mitra-peninsula attracts a great many visitors. Tourists are expected to camp only on the allotted site and to cause minimum disturbance to the scientists and wildlife. The campsite lies to the east of the village. From the pier you follow the main road through the settlement to the junction further up a gentle slope. To the right is the runway and the domes of the former ESRO-station; the road to the left leads to the campsite. Apart from the 10.-nkr levy on all visitors to Ny Ålesund the campsite is free; however there is only a primitive toilet and litter container. A nearby stream provides water. Camping is not permitted elsewhere on the private land of the King's Bay Kull Company nor near the bird sanctuary close to the shore on either side of the settlement.

The beaches on both sides of the settlement, to the right of the pier on the northwest and immediately after the last buildings on the east, are bird sanctuaries. Access is strictly forbidden to these areas. Tourists should be careful to avoid all disturbance to the birds here, and make sure they use binoculars from a safe distance.

In contrast to Longyearbyen, this is a scientific community and not a tourist resort. Avoid any disruption to installations and equipment. As many cruise ships land here in the summer this isolated community can become quite lively at this time.

Sveagruva

This small settlement was founded as a Swedish coal-mining community in 1917, but by 1925 mining had ceased and it was later purchased by SNSK. The small Akseløya which almost blocks the estuary of Van Mijenfjord is responsible for the prolonged presence of drift-ice in the fjord. Sveagruva, situated at the top of the Van Mijenfjord, is therefore not very accessible for most of the year.

In 1944 during the Second World War it was destroyed in a German U-boat attack. SNSK re-opened the coal-mine after the war but had to close it again in 1949.

Renewed geological surveys of the coal deposits around Sveagruva resulted in some experimental mining operations at the beginning of the '70s. In the mid-'80s it was extensively modernised and expanded. Following the dramatic drop in world coal prices and the resulting need for heavy subsidies coal production in Sveagruva ceased again in July 1987.

A maintenance team of 11 men keep the mine operational as there is still potential for mining the extensive seam in the future. It is still being debated whether the central field, which is at present being explored in the mountain range north of Svea, should be exploited from Svea to the south or from the north (see chapter on Longyearbyen). If the northern approach is opened it would require a road to be built from Longyearbyen across the yet untouched hinterland. The road could have untold consequences on the balance of nature. If in the future there is a need for extensive mining activities then Svea might be a better centre of exploitation from the conservation point of view, especially as the mine here, with its own deposits, can be opened again at any time.

Apart from the possibility of resuming coal mining at some time in the future there are also plans to develop

Sveagruva into a scientific research and educational establishment, utilising the existing buildings.

An excellent canteen and first aid centre are still used. An up-to-date telecommunications system maintains contact with the outside world. A unique feature of Svea is the small private air strip in the middle of town where lights stop traffic whenever a plane takes off or lands. The town, built for a much larger community, has a deserted feel to it. Everything is well looked after but the people are gone.

There are occasional supply flights from Longyearbyen in SNSK's twin engined plane. Occasionally helicopters land and freight ships bring extra goods. Passenger ships usually do not visit Svea.

Hornsund: Little Poland
Unlike the Norwegian and Soviet settlements the Polish research station on the northern shore of the Hornsund is little known. About 12 people stay all year round and some 15 scientists join them during the summer; the population is then larger than Sveagruva. Its inhabitants affectionately refer to Hornsund as *Little Poland*.

There is a long tradition of Arctic research by the Poles which has its origins in scientific studies of Siberia by some educated Poles who had the misfortune of being deported to Siberian camps during the Tsar's reign of Poland. Some of the first scientific reports of the Arctic were written by these Polish convicts.

Six Polish expeditions visited Spitsbergen in the early 1930s. They concentrated particularly on the previously neglected, heavily glaciated southern end of the main island. A number of place names still bear witness of these activities (Polakkbreen, Pilsudski etc). There was a break of about 20 years in Polish involvement with Spitsbergen due to World War II and the subsequent Stalin years.

The Polish station was established at Hornsund in 1957/58 and was, until the recent political changes in East Europe, a rare chance for Polish scientists to carry out research in a free international environment. As the Polish coast on the Baltic sea is heavily polluted with industrial waste, for Polish marine biologists this station offers almost the only chance to study relatively unpolluted coastal waters. The Poles are therefore keen to foster and maintain good relations with the Norwegian governor and the Norsk Polarinstitutt. Despite the considerable distance separating Hornsund and Longyearbyen, Polish-Norwegian relations are close, warm, relaxed and trusting.

There are many long-term projects carried on in the areas of geophysics, seismology, meteorology and the ionosphere (northern lights!) as well as one-off projects concerning geology, glaciers, geomorphology, marine biology, oceanography and cartography. Maintaining this station during the present economic plight of Poland is not easy and work often has to be undertaken in difficult circumstances. The visitor should be considerate and not exploit the hospitality. Apart from the Poles, scientists from various countries use the station; they are always greeted as welcomed guests.

The Norwegian stations

Apart from the three previously described settlements, Norway maintains three other stations all year round.

One peculiarity of interest to tourists and philatelists is that all three stations have their own postmark. The three are:

— **Isfjord Radio** (Kap Linné): The station of the Norwegian telecommunications authority Norsk Tele, that serves the telegraphic and radio requirements of the area. There is a five-man crew. A large area surrounding the station is a bird-sanctuary/nature reserve with severe restrictions on visitors!

— **Bjørnøya** (Bear Island): Meterological station, 12-man crew (1985). Despite its remote location an amazingly large number of tourists call here by ship or yacht. There are some souvenirs for sale. Nearby is the Hammerfesthuset, the oldest house on Svalbard, dating from 1823. There is a small museum in the station. Attempts to mine the local coal-resources were abandoned a long time ago. The island was discovered by Willem Barents in 1596. An expedition member shot a polar bear here which is the origin of the island's name. (Alistair Maclean immortalised the island with his thriller *Bear Island*.) Landing on the island is often difficult as there are no sheltered bays, the cliffs are mostly sheer and there is fog for much of the time.

— **Hopen**: The remotest of all the stations serves meterological purposes. It was originally established by the German armed forces during World War II as a weather station. The Norwegians retained the station and later expanded it.

TOURISM

ILLUSIONS, EXPECTATIONS AND CONTRADICTIONS

Before dealing with the practical aspects of a journey to Spitsbergen it is appropriate to think about motives, expectations and attitudes towards this Arctic destination.

"Spitsbergen is not a destination for a traveller" — these were the first words I received from the Norwegian Consulate a few years ago when I was preparing for my first visit here. Though the islands have been opened to tourism for a number of years there is still some truth in this statement when compared with other northern destinations such as the Faroes, Iceland or Greenland.

The visitor must be prepared to find few if any conveniences even within some of the settlements. Even in Longyearbyen it is advisable not to rely completely on local supplies. Whilst you may be surprised to find an item you had not expected to see for sale, it can also happen that a simple pair of rubber boots is not available

in your size and the next delivery is not for two weeks.

Considering the total population is only 3,500 with just 1,055 residents in Longyearbyen, there is a surprisingly wide variety of goods and services on offer. Many services, designed for the local people, are offered free or at the same favourable prices to visitors.

Today at least the basic tourist necessities are catered for in Longyearbyen: accommodation, cafeteria/ restaurant, shops for food, souvenirs, etc., but tourism still plays a very modest part in the economy.

Another thing to bear in mind is that facilities are often not duplicated on Spitsbergen. If, for example, the service building at the camp site is closed for repairs, then there is no other possibility for visitors to have daily showers. If a certain commodity is sold out then stocks are unavailable until the next shipment, which might not be due for several weeks. In the summer of 1989 the airport was closed for four weeks for urgent repair work to the runway and only a few smaller planes were able to land. Such shortcomings are known about in advance by the tour operators but independent travellers are severely hampered by such inconveniences.

Again and again I encounter visitors who expect an untouched paradise but with all the home comforts they are accustomed to. On Svalbard I am frequently struck by how deeply our age of artificial pleasures, of thrills through television without the risks of hardship, have pervaded our thinking and acting. So many people set out for the Arctic, tired of the routine and boredom of everyday life, longing for challenge and excitement but taking with them the video generation's attitudes.

Outside the settlements life is not like a game which can be switched off when it becomes too hard or dangerous. The hardships are real and ever present. It is not possible to 'do' the Arctic like some gigantic computer game, expecting the romance of old-fashioned trapper cabins with a hot stove and a winter's storm raging outside or becoming a heroic polar explorer without the reality of the hardships. These are fairy-tale dreams. However, every newcomer to Svalbard probably has such contradictory expectations. Where else on earth, if it isn't here, can one expect to find one last lost paradise? As with other exotic, unknown places the imagination runs wild picturing an untouched land but with the security of comfort and easy access.

Disappointment in such dreams is inevitable. Even Svalbard, untouched though it is, shows traces of man's activities almost everywhere, from litter on the shores to air pollution in the skies, from caterpillar tracks to a beer bottle carelessly discarded. Compared to anywhere else in Europe these traces are minute but nevertheless a disappointment when it was virgin land that the visitor longed for. The comfort offered may be less than what is taken for granted at home but sufficient for communities to live here and for visitors to return. The sight of the modern airport at Longyearbyen, the mining facilities and a modern settlement with youngsters watching the latest videos and riding around on motor-bikes, is far from the romance of a trapper's life.

These unrealistic or romantic expectations can lead to frustrations and unfair criticism. Certainly the sight of a messy old drilling site, rusting cans or caterpillar tracks are disillusioning. Before condemning 'industry' or 'the Norwegians' or 'tourists' for many undisputed sins we should consider the age of the rubbish. The Arctic preserves everything mercilessly: litter remains for decades unlike ours at home which soon gets covered by a tangle of weeds. However in recent years ecological awareness has improved considerably. An abandoned drilling site from 1989 (Haketangen) looks very different from one of 20 or 30 years ago (Berzeliusdalen). We should also stop to think how well we have cared for our own homelands. Perhaps it is just the frustration of knowing that at the end of the 20th century there are no longer any untouched paradises left on earth.

Certainly constructive criticism can be valuable in preventing or at least repairing damage that has already occurred in Spitsbergen, especially at a time when tourism is being considered as an expanding source of income. Tourists come mainly because of the unspoilt nature of the land and massive litter (such as the stream from Mine 7 into Adventdalen filled with plastic cans etc) or the appalling remains of Soviet drilling activities on Fuglefjellet do nothing to advertise Spitsbergen as a clean place. Fair, constructive remarks may help to reduce such problems.

The visitor must also set a positive example by bringing all litter back from the field, avoid disturbing animals and plants and respecting the rules of Spitsbergen. One such rule is that the emergency shelters which are generally left unlocked are not for casual use without special permission. Do not abuse the trust that is offered by people in this country. It would also help if visitors showed their agreement to the present tourist policy of not creating roads, or marked paths or tourist cabins in the hinterland which would completely alter the wilderness.

Up till now Spitsbergen has managed to preserve its own way of life, unlike many typical tourist resorts. Do respect the local's interests. This is a normal community of family, social and cultural activities. The residents may not appreciate hikers mistaking the cafeteria for some primitive cabin in the outback, leaving on their muddy hiking boots or spreading out clothes to dry.

Remember that you are visiting communities whose services are primarily there for the residents and not set up for tourists, though visitors profit from many of the facilities.

I have already said that the lack of tourist infrastructure outside the settlements is the best protection of the Arctic. It is exactly because there are no roads or bridges over every stream, or cabins in the countryside that it is still so unspoiled. If such a construction programme was undertaken the archipelago would be ruined within a few short years by the arrival of masses of tourists. In a previous publication I described routes to visitors. Despite the fact that I gave warnings about the ever-changing landscape hikers assumed that these described routes were therefore 'easy'. This is never the case in the Arctic, and you should always be aware of this. Any marking of routes is likely to attract ill-equipped hikers which will inevitably lead to more serious problems. So suffer the hardships you encounter instead of complaining and discourage the Norwegians from opening this special place to mass tourism. This is the only way of preserving this magnificent Arctic country for our successors and the few who are dedicated enough to enjoy its harsh solitude and grand landscape. Let us be able to leave behind the gadgets of civilization which distract us from experiencing our environment directly, sensitively and respectfully.

Following this introduction are notes on the possibilities of travel to Svalbard with additional advice for special groups of visitors.

POSSIBILITIES FOR VISITING THE ISLANDS

In this chapter I would like to elaborate on the various ways to get to know Spitsbergen as a tourist.

Despite the difficulties of tourism here there are still a large number of options for travellers. Contrary to other more southern destinations with their well developed infrastructure that enable the individual to travel freely wherever he wishes, tourism here is almost exclusively (95%) organised by several international tour operators. Even many travellers who would not use the services of a tour operator for other destinations prefer to join a tour when heading for Spitsbergen. The reason for this is simple — cost, and the lack of Arctic experience. A tour operator can distribute costs over many participants during a season whereas the individual is unable to do so. However there are still a few private expeditions each year and though the number is low I have included a section on equipment (weapons, tents ...) which may be of interest only to this small group. There is also additional information towards the end of this chapter for specialists. However this book cannot possibly replace practical experience and knowledge of local conditions.

Read the brochures of the various tour organizers carefully to picture what they have to offer. Those who exclude a cruise through prejudice will miss the cheapest way of getting a short impression of the west coast. Those who think trekking a waste of energy, carting around heavy loads, will never feel the intense experience of being close to nature and exploring the land at first hand. The type of trip you choose is worth thinking over carefully. Any good travel agent will have up to date information. Check the details to compare prices and destinations visited. If in doubt contact the author.

Tour operators

At present few tour operators offer trips to Spitsbergen. They include:

Spitzbergen Tours Andreas Umbreit Dammstrasse 36, D-2300, Kiel 1. Tel. -49 431 91678. (See page 118)
The author of this guide and acknowledged expert on Spitsbergen with the largest selection of tours: trekking, short-stay, ship tours 2-17 days, special arrangements.

Arctic Experience 29 Nork Way, Banstead, Surrey SM7 1B, Tel. 0737 362321, or the Flatt Lodge, Bewcastle, near Carlisle,Cumbria CA6 6PH, Tel. 06978 356. (See page 3)
Specialising in the Arctic, they offer sledging, ship tours of varying duration and trekking.

Regent Holidays (UK) Ltd, 13 Small Street, Bristol BS1 1DE. Tel. 0272 211711. (See page 31)
Cruises, cruise and camp expeditions, trips based at Barentsburg or Longyearbyen.

Itineraries change, so for up to date information contact the tour operator.

Cruises

A cruise ship voyage is a combination of taking a holiday in a good or even exclusive hotel, with all its social pleasures, and at the same time getting an impression of foreign countries.

Of the 22,000 visitors to Spitsbergen each year about 16,000 come on board cruise ships. About 30 cruises call at Spitsbergen every summer combining visits to a number of countries (Orkneys, Faroes, Iceland, Greenland etc). Most of the longer voyages go north via Iceland and the lonely Norwegian volcanic island of Jan Mayen, then head for the edge of the pack-ice before reaching the northwest coast of Spitsbergen. Shorter cruises go from the mainland of Norway to Spitsbergen. The duration of stay in Spitsbergen's waters varies, but is hardly ever longer than two days.

Most ships call at Kongsfjord or Magdalena Bay in the far north west, especially famous for its glaciers which slope dramatically down into the sea. There tourists are brought ashore by landing craft, as long as weather and ice conditions permit. Some of these cruises include other landings on the coast at Krossfjord, Isfjord (Barentsburg, Longyearbyen) and its easternmost branch, Tempelfjord (Kapp Schoultz). It is advisable to study planned itineraries carefully as there are considerable differences in the routes offered.

As there are several categories of cabin offered on these large ships and each ship has its own distinctive style, catering for those who require luxury to those wishing to participate in an informative natural history cruise, the choice for the visitor is very wide, much wider than any other way of reaching Spitsbergen. Accordingly, the prices range from £1,000 to £10,000 for a 14 day cruise. Surprisingly, though, some of these cruises are among the cheapest means of visiting the archipelago. The cruise ships offer the possibility of visiting a number of nordic destinations in relative comfort and in a single journey.

In spite of the *Maxim Gorki* incident in 1989 when the ship ran into difficulties and all the passengers had to be rescued in a magnificent effort by the coast guards, safety standards on these ships are very high. In fact probably no other means of visiting the Arctic carries less risk.

The season for such nordic cruises is from early June to the second half of August. In Spitsbergen the earlier part of this period allows you to experience the midnight sun which is at its highest on June 22nd; when the weather is good the sky remains bright blue both day and night. On land the snow has only just started to melt so most of the lower parts of the mountains will still be snow covered contrasting magnificently with the dark rock walls above. Drifting ice and fjord ice can be a problem at any time of the season, guaranteeing that a strict itinerary can never be adhered to — but this is part of the Arctic experience! Watching the bizarre shapes of small icebergs and drifting ice in a landscape often shrouded in a mysterious layer of mist is an impression that one can only get in these polar regions.

Good weatherproof clothes are needed for the shore landings and a strong pair of rubber boots with warm socks as the terrain is often muddy. Wind and rainproof clothes are also necessary on board ship, including hat and gloves against the cold. The tour organisers will offer advice on clothing necessary for the social events on board.

In 1990 summer came late to Spitsbergen. Here at Tempelfjord the ice has only just broken up in July.

Unlike other forms of travel here, there is no problem with the use of electronic equipment. Batteries can be recharged (make sure you have the correct adaptors and plugs). Even video cameras can be used and kept safe in a warm cabin, quite different from conditions on a trekking tour!

If you are interested in longer cruises along Spitsbergen's fascinating coast you might consider a trip on one of the smaller coastal vessels which operate here during the summer (see following section).

I have produced an annual list of all the nordic cruises I know which include Spitsbergen. The list contains more cruises than those offered from the United Kingdom and gives ships, dates, board languages, detailed prices, destinations and addresses of the main agencies selling these tours. The list is available for $4.00 or £2.00 postal order from Andreas Umbreit, Dammstr.36, D-2300 Kiel 1 or by bank transfer to my postgiro account 630307-201, Postgiroamt Hamburg, West Germany.

The following notes on coastal areas cover the places generally visited by cruises or small vessels.

Most cruise ships head first for the border of the pack ice and approach Spitsbergen from the north. Accordingly I begin my description from the Wijdefjord.

Key: **Northwest Coast**

A Wijdefjord			
B Mosselbukta			
C Gråhuken			
D Bockfjord			
E Moffen	L Krossfjord		
F Reinsdyrflya	M Kongsford	R Kapp Starostin	W Grumant
G Fair Haven	N Engelskbukta	S Festningen	X Adventfjord
H Amsterdamøya	O Sarstangen,	T Grønfjord	Y Kapp Thorsden
I Danskøya	Forlandsundet	U Trygghamna/	Z Billefjord
J Magdalenafjord	P Kap Linné	Safe Harbour	AA Sassendalen
K Hamburgbukta	Q Linnévannet	V Colesbukta	AB Tempelfjord

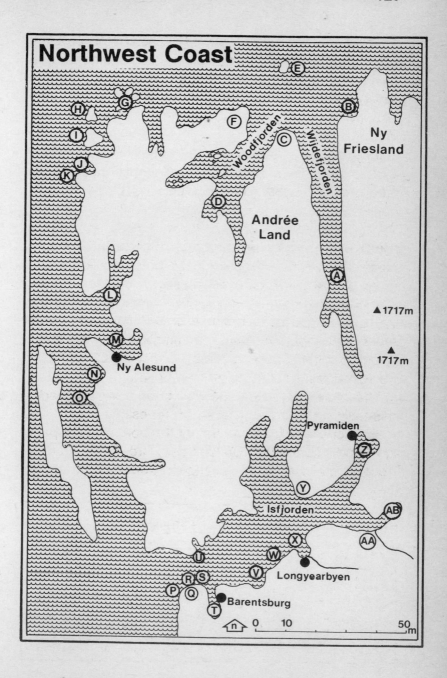

Wijdefjord (A): Wijdefjord at 110km long is one of the longest fjords on Svalbard. It is separated from the Isfjord by a 20km wide isthmus. Andréeland to the west is an area of Alpine mountain ranges and valleys. Its southern part is the driest on Spitsbergen where the shifting permanent snow level is sometimes above 800m. To the east the land is ice covered in Ny Friesland and folded into huge rugged mountain ranges towards the south where two of the highest mountains Newtontoppen and Perriertoppen (both 1717m) dominate the landscape. In Austfjord is one of the last remaining trapper stations near the impressive ice front of Mittag-Leffler-Glacier where the fjord ends.

Mosselbukta (B): In 1872/73 the Finnish-Swedish scientist Nordenskiöld was the first to set up a winter station here. Surprised by the ice, the crews on the expedition ship *Polhem* and the two supporting ships were obliged to set up base; a total of 67 men overwintered here. They named the base Polhem and from here Nordenskiöld explored much of the Nordaustlandet. Remains of the base can still be seen. Today only one trapper has his hut here.

Gråhuken (C): Named after the grey Devonian sediments, this is where six Norwegian hunter vessels were trapped by ice in 1872. Seventeen crew members made their way south in two small boats to Kapp Thordsen in Isfjord only to perish from scurvy the following year. Thirty eight more were rescued when the ice retreated and were taken safely home to Norway. Two sailors, still caught by the ice, made a make-shift shelter from two upturned boats, but they too died of scurvy.

Bockfjord (D): Its unique feature is the warm springs (about 24°C) on the western side of the fjord close to the extinct cone of a quaternary volcano. These springs are all that remain of former volcanic activity on Spitsbergen.

Moffen (E): A flat, ring-shaped pebble island with a lagoon in the middle, the island is now a walrus reserve and approach is restricted to 300m. Recently the colony seems to have diminished whereas other coastal observations show an increase in the walrus population.

Reinsdyrflya (F): Flat large peninsula inhabited by almost 1000 reindeer. Much of the beach is coloured a deep red. During the last war there was a German weather station here.

Fair Haven (G): A sheltered sound between the tiny islands of Fugleøya, Fuglesangen, Klovninger and Norskeøyane where the 17th century whaling fleets took haven. On Ytre Norskøya there was once a Dutch whaling station.

Amsterdamøya (H): Together with Danskøya this is mainly of historical interest. The Dutch Smeerenburg (blubber town) flourished here in the 17th century, the largest of all the whaling stations on Spitsbergen. Remains of the processing ovens can still be seen. A visit will give a better insight into the harsh conditions of those times than any history book.

Danskøya (I): This, too, was a whaling base and many graves scatter the ground, some reopened by heavy frost. Like all other historic remains dated prior to 1900 these graves are strictly protected as historical monuments. Virgohamna (Virgin Harbour) on the island was the base of Andrée's and Wellmann's attempts by balloon and zeppelin to reach the north pole.

Magdalenafjord (J): One of the most beautiful of all the fjords. Steep rock faces tower up from the water, edged by the surrounding rugged mountains and interrupted by several glaciers. Half-way up the fjord is a sheltered point where most cruise ships dock. A memorial reminds visitors of the whalers and sailors who lost their lives.

Hamburgbukta (K): A small shallow bay where German whalers from the city of Hamburg had their base.

Krossfjord (L): Cross Bay and neighbouring King's Bay are two of the destinations visited by cruises. The landscape is impressive with its small side fjords and large glaciers (Lilliehöökbreen, Tinayrebreen) which frequently break into icebergs that are seen drifting out into the fjord. To the west is Ebeltoftbay where old whalers' graves have recently been excavated.

Kongsford (M): The landscape is dominated by the Tre Kroner (three crowns) rising above the Kongsbreen. They are named after the three nordic kingdoms of Nora, Svea and Dana. Several small islands in the fjord are bird reserves where basking seals can often be seen. A visit to Ny Ålesund, the northernmost settlement in the world, is often incorporated in tours (see chapter on Ny Ålesund). Another landing is New London on Blomstrandhalvøya. Here an Englishman, Mansfield, started a small settlement and opened a quarry to make his fortune from the local marble, only to find it was rendered worthless by the many cracks in the stone.

Engelskbukta (N): Here English whalers had a base, though as the old English name for the settlement was Comfortless Bay it was probably not their favourite site.

Sarstangen, Forlandsundet (O): Only the flat bottomed coastal vessels can pass through the shallow Forland Sound (a depth of 5m beyond Sarstangen promontory). The mountain range on Prins Karls Forlandet rises up more than 1000m. The sheer rock face is interrupted by ice cascades and glaciers.

Kap Linné (P): Isfjord radio and weather station is based on this cape. The surrounding land is a bird sanctuary.

Linnévannet (Q): The second largest lake on the islands is wonderfully situated between two rugged mountain ranges. Geologists find the surrounding countryside of interest as one of the few areas where under ground springs melt the permafrost. Some possible artifacts have been recorded from Linnévannet suggesting occupation by early man in the so called Atlanticum period following the last ice age, but the consensus of opinion now is that these 'tools' are coincidental products of nature. Where the small river from the lake enters the fjord a former Russian hunter settlement, Russekeila, has recently been excavated.

Kapp Starostin (R): The cape is named after the last Russian monk to live on Spitsbergen who died in 1826 after 39 winters on the islands.

Festningen (S): Like a fortress wall the hard sedimentary Cretaceous sandstone was forced up by Tertiary folding along the west coast and reaches out into the fjord.

Nearby, footprints of the huge Iguanodon were discovered, a replica of which can be seen in the museum at Longyearbyen.

Grønfjord (T): There have been whaling stations on either side of the fjord up to this century; remains of one can still be seen just outside Barentsburg. Grønfjord, also known formerly as Green Harbour, was where the first telegraph station was installed and remained until 1930.

Trygghamna/Safe Harbour (U): The narrow fjord is the first sheltered bay on the north side of Isfjord and was once a base for whalers and walrus hunters.

Colesbukta (V): The Soviet settlement of Colesbukta was originally the port for the coal mines at Grumantbyen and was of considerable importance until the mines closed in the '50s. A railway connected the two settlements, the tracks of which can still be followed until their disappearance into an ice-blocked tunnel in the cliffs. North of here at Rusanovodden, the Soviets have erected a small museum named after the Russian Geologist W.A. Rusanov who, in 1912, made the first Soviet land claims.

Grumant (W): A former Soviet mining settlement, rather difficult to reach, nestled in a narrow valley between steep cliffs. It is now abandoned and is an untidy mass of crumbling buildings.

Adventfjord (X): The main place of interest in the small bay on the southern side of the Isfjord is Longyearbyen, the capital (see chapter on settlements). All the names starting with 'Advent...' probably have their origin in a British 18th century whaling ship *Adventure*. At the entrance to the bay on the western side is *Vestpynten* (Westpoint), where we see the big parabolic antennas of the radio relay system that connects Isfjord Radio at Kapp Linné (P) and Longyearbyen. Small private cabins can be seen along the shore. Hotelneset, a coastal plain, extends from Vestpynten between the shore and the steep sides of Plateauberget. It is so named because of a hotel operated by a Norwegian shipping company at the turn of the century. The airport, campsite, coal storage depot and port now occupy the plain. A Norwegian Second World War cannon now stands behind the storage area as a memorial.

The wide delta of Adventelva (Advent river) extends further into the fjord each year as detritus is swept down from inland. The last 15km of the river are muddy and in summer impossible to cross, there being no bridge. The apparently close eastern shore of Adventfjord (approx 3km across at Longyearbyen) is in practice a good day's hike away (20-30kms). On this eastern side can be seen remains of two former mining settlements.

Hjorthamn was first mined by Norwegians in 1916-1921 but was not very profitable due to difficult topography. The mine entrance, high up on the mountain, and remains of a funicular are still to be seen. In 1929 musk ox were introduced from Greenland (see chapter on mammals) but the experiment was unsuccessful. The settlement therefore became known as Moskushamn (Musk harbour). Some of the cabins are still used by local people as during the winter months the Adventfjord is passable by motor-sledge.

Advent City was established by Englishmen and the coal exploited at the beginning of the century but soon abandoned. Buildings were later transferred to Hjorthamn and only a few foundations remain. A new telecommunications relay station has recently been set up in the area. More leisure cabins can be seen here and out towards Revneset (Fox promontory).

Kapp Thordsen (Y): The cape is best known for the *Svenskhuset* (Swedish house) a large building erected in 1872 by a Swedish company intending to exploit the phosphate deposits, another well intentioned project that failed. The house played a sad role in the drama of Gråhuken (see (C) above) and was later used as base for the Swedish expedition of 1882-83. The building is a national monument preserved as a memorial to early mining pioneers and to those of the first scientific explorations.

Billefjord (Z): The northernmost part of the Isfjord. To the east is the huge Nordenskiöld glacier which descends into the fjord and Pyramiden, the second largest Soviet settlement (see chapter on settlements). Nearby is Skansbukta and Skansen mountain recognisable by its impressive rock face of alternating layers of white and dark sediment. At the bottom of the scree slopes, the remains of an ill-fated mine (tunnel entrance, rails, building) still can be seen. On the other side of Skansbukta, there is an interesting old and decaying trapper cabin.

Sassendalen (AA): This is the valley of the largest river of the islands. The delta extends far into the fjord. Sir Martin Conway followed this valley at the start of the first attempt to cross the island. On the eastern side of the estuary is Fredheim (Home of Peace), the home of the most famous 20th century trapper Hilmar Nois. He spent 50 summers and 39 winters on Spitsbergen sometimes accompanied by his wife. Today the cabin is maintained by the governor and used as an official guest house and base for scientific field work.

Tempelfjord (AB): One of the most spectacular places with steep rock walls ascending 600m up from the water's edge. Templet mountain dominates the northern side of the fjord. Several pillars have been eroded into the horizontal sedimentary rock face, Skiltvakten (sentry) being the most impressive. The fjord ends in the joint ice front of Tunabreen and Von Post breen. The latter glacier is retreating but Tunabreen is an impressive ice wall which occasionally breaks into icebergs which then drift slowly out into the fjord. Some cruise-ships anchor at Kapp Schoultz on the southern side of the fjord where the remains of a short-lived mine — rails, funicular, mine entrance up on the slope — can be found.

Trips in small coastal vessels

Since the Hurtigrute, Norway's coastal ship service, ceased regular summer service to Svalbard in 1983 there have been no regular passenger ship services to Spitsbergen and freight ships are not allowed to carry passengers. However, each summer a few small coastal vessels are transferred from the Norwegian mainland and elsewhere to the islands. Occasionally passengers may be accepted on the often rough crossing in June or on their return in September. In 1990, nine such small vessels operated in Spitsbergen's waters during the summer, offering up to 46 berths. This capacity proved to be a massive over-estimation of the actual demand for transport. One of them that tried to offer a regular service between Ny Ålesund and Longyearbyen twice a week had to give up during the season and some of the others were seen for long periods just waiting at the pier, hoping for the appearance of masses of independent tourists. Only those with prearranged full charters for most of the season by tour operators, scientists, etc. managed to operate profitably. Once again this proved that the number of independently travelling tourists is too small in Spitsbergen to install regular shipping lines for them, whereas the number of ships under charter by professional tour operators has risen continuously. For 1991, at least five such small coastal vessels with 20-46 berths will be chartered by international tour operators for the summer season, to carry out their tour programmes. The participants are on board for 2-16 days with frequent landings. These coastal cruise arrangements should be booked in advance via travel agents; only rarely is there space available on these cruises for last minute bookings on the spot — if such bookings are accepted at all.

About three more small coastal vessels take over other charter traffic, for instance scientific expeditions, journalist groups, etc. In 1990, the daily charters for such a ship varied between 16,000.-nkr (11 berths) to 50,000.-nkr (46 berths). In the event of these ships having days without charters they may offer in Longyearbyen day cruises in the Isfjord lasting about seven hours. In recent years, such occasional extra day cruises were sold for about 600.-nkr per passenger. However, a minimum number of participants is required and as these short cruises fill only spare capacity, they are offered usually just a few days before departure. Furthermore, these day-trips are mostly restricted to the Isfjord. The visitor who has not booked a tour in advance therefore cannot expect to find transport to a certain destination within a few days at a low price after his arrival in Spitsbergen, especially if he wants to leave the Isfjord.

To avoid disappointment and loss of time in Longyearbyen, waiting for a chance stand-by, it is advisable to book a ship tour in Spitsbergen before you leave home, either by joining the fixed programmes of one of the tour operators or by making a special arrangement, for instance by getting a group together (charter rates mentioned above). See also page 125.

Accommodation on these small boats is basic, quite unlike the luxury of a cruise ship, but they offer a unique opportunity to experience Arctic conditions more fully.

Such journeys last from 3-18 days, the shorter ones concentrating on the northwest coast (see description above). Some of the longer tours attempt to sail round the archipelago, not always possible every year. Prices range between £1,250 to £2,700 from northern Norway, depending on the number of days on board.

The following are two examples of tours offered on the British market in 1990:

3 days voyage by coastal ship plus added accommodation in Longyearbyen (3 days) £1646 return London:
First day arrive in Longyearbyen, transfer to accommodation, sight-seeing including visit to Svalbard museum. Next day excursion to nearby Adventdalen, then reboard vessel. The route leads to the main Soviet settlement of Barentsburg (guided tour). Then the ship leaves for Isfjord and turns north through the Forland sound to Magdalenafjord, Danskøya, the northern drifting ice, Woodfjord and Bockfjord on the north coast. Back via Ny Ålesund and Krossfjord. After three days return to Longyearbyen. As no one sleeps much during this trip

— who wants to miss the spectacular coastal scenery? — the last day is appreciated for resting and a farewell dinner. Next day the plane leaves Spitsbergen.

14-18 days with several different routes to choose along the coast, including attempts at circling the main island. Lectures on board and daily land excursions. £2237-3166 return London (depending on length and accommodation). These trips are well-worthwhile for those with a deep interest in the Arctic.

Programmes, ships and operators change each year. In the past some operators have failed to fulfil their promises and have plunged their participants into Arctic adventures of a most unpleasant nature. When choosing a tour operator it would be advisable to contact a specialist in this field.

Motorized rubber boats

As from 1989 a rule became effective which demands a passenger certificate for the Arctic for any vessel used to transport people. Such a certificate is unlikely to be given for an open rubber inflatable dinghy. The rule was triggered by the risk-taking activities of some tour operators. Before the discouragement of such tours the use of powerful engined open boats had become increasingly popular.

Trekking

Despite the over-use of the word 'trekking', I use it here to refer only to longer hiking tours where distances from camp to camp are covered on foot. Groups continue along their route and set up camp at suitable places. This does not exclude the possibility of spending an additional day or two at one site to rest or explore the immediate surroundings. Thus large distances are covered.

Longyearbyen is well situated as a starting point for a hiking tour, apart from the fact that it is here that the international airport is situated. The surrounding Nordenskiøldland has less ice cover than other parts of the archipelago. In spite of the proximity to a settlement, the Arctic conditions and the lack of infrastructure are demanding enough to deter the comfort-seeking tourist. Thus, within half a day's hike from Longyearbyen, you can experience the solitude of this extraordinary wilderness.

However, because there are no marked routes and maps are not entirely reliable in an ever changing topography, trekking in this wilderness with its numerous Arctic peculiarities (permafrost, cunningly camouflaged morasses, wild glacial streams, muddy moraine fields etc) requires practical experience with the Arctic and knowledge of the terrain, otherwise time, energy and the limited food being carried will be wasted. The necessity for carrying the correct gun, signal pistol, ammunition etc. often is a persuasive influence on otherwise competent hikers to travel with a trekking tour operator. Most of these problems are then solved. The Nordenskiøldland and some adjoining areas make countless interesting tours possible, from a day long hike to a four week trek. Hiking with a tent, is, in my opinion, the best way to get to know the fascinating Arctic. Since you have to work to cross the area on foot, it is a more intense and direct experience than seeing nature as a backdrop while passing in a motor vehicle.

The main problem with hiking is the weight of the backpack which each hiker must carry. For this reason

I have established storage depots for food and fuel for my own tours where members of my groups can replenish supplies. On a 17 day trekking tour this makes a difference in rucksack weight of up to 15 kilos, thus considerably improving the chance of enjoying the tour.

Hiking tours in Spitsbergen require you to be in good physical shape and surefooted, but otherwise no serious mountain climbing or ice experience is necessary as long as one avoids unknown climbing routes or glacier crossings. Having said this any participant should be aware of the extreme conditions under which they will be living and take their own personal preparation seriously. Make sure that you read the information on the demands of the tour (distance covered by day, weight of backpack, number of days) and make sure that you have done something comparable before without difficulty. A difference of a few kilometres or a few kilos is something that should be taken seriously! If in any doubt test yourself on a realistic cross-country tour at home with a night in the field with all the equipment listed by your tour operator. All equipment should be realistically tested before you leave home.

As only a few people practise constant serious physical training the change to the demands of a trekking tour are considerable. Therefore preparatory fitness exercise is very advisable. Most important is the circulation and the leg and feet muscles. An excellent training is cross-country running on uneven terrain, perfect preparation for Spitsbergen's pathless wilderness.

Once out in the wilderness the group must always keep within sight of each other and take the advice of the experienced guide to avoid any unnecessary mishaps.

Apart from my own programme (write to me for this year's schedule — address on page 118) most other trekking groups are organized by private mountaineering clubs which may sometimes offer specialized rock- or ice-climbing tours.

Motor-sledge (skidoo) tours

During the last few years skidoo tours have been offered. The most suitable time is March-April before the thaw, however it is still very cold at this time (see climatic table) and special insulated suits are essential. The tours require an experienced guide, not only for technical repairs but with a knowledge of the terrain. Safety equipment (ropes, gun, signals etc) and emergency bivouacs need to be taken on the sledges. For 1990 such a skidoo tour of eight nights in Spitsbergen (hostel/tent) cost £1700 return London.

Short stays

The number of visitors coming for a short stay of 2-5 days has increased over the past years. Regular flights from Tromsø, Norway are booked up well in advance especially by visiting relatives during holiday periods and by various tour operators in the summer.

Short stays are usually restricted to Longyearbyen. Those coming independently should stay longer to make up for time lost due to a lack of knowledge of local conditions.

Longyearbyen offers simple accommodation, a canteen and restaurant. A stroll around town including a visit to the museum takes about 2-4 hours. Guided tours round one of the mines are offered by the coal company. For the inexperienced visitor hiking is not encouraged as it is unwise to travel out of sight of the settlements without prior experience with Arctic terrain and without a suitable weapon and shooting experience. The immediate surroundings of Longyearbyen with the possibility for pathless but not difficult walks are restricted on the one side by the fjord and the other by steep mountain slopes. Within this limited area the typical excursions lead to the moraine of the Longyear glacier and to the edge of Plateauberget to view the town in its narrow valley. You can hire a bicycles to follow the gravel road into Adventdalen (to Mine 7, about 11km) or to the coal port, camp site/airport and Vestpynten (about 7km). There are no other roads leaving Longyearbyen. All these activities in and around the town fill about 2-3 days (provided the weather is suitable). The Arctic wilderness begins abruptly beyond the few roads and buildings.

Visitors who want to use a short stay with its limited time efficiently may be better off with a guided tour. This guarantees interesting and tested routes for day trips into the pathless surrounding areas and allows day excursions further into the wilderness than is advisable without the local experience and background information of the guide. The guide can help with reserving day cruises on the fjord on stand-by basis (before the arrival of the traveller in Longyearbyen) or with organising a sightseeing flight — a fantastic though expensive additional highlight of such a short stay in Spitsbergen. Due to the modest size of land tourism in Spitsbergen, there is no organised guide service by locals. Unlike most countries, there is no native population in need of work. If you arrive in Longyearbyen and need a guide you could try the Governor's office, but are unlikely to be successful.

I arrange such short stay offers for 2½ and 5½ days in Spitsbergen, including regular flights from/to Tromso (northern Norway), prices starting at 485/590 pounds (1991). Short stays in Longyearbyen require no particularly unusual equipment: solid hiking boots, wind and rain-proof solid clothes, some extra warm clothes (pullover, gloves, cap, warm socks), small pack for food etc. on day-trips and a warm sleeping-bag if camping.

Night Charter flights

During the summer there are trips from Oslo to the land of the midnight sun, Spitsbergen. You land shortly after midnight at Longyearbyen and are met by a bus which tours the town and allows a visit to the Svalbard museum. At around four o'clock the plane returns to Oslo. About 4,000 visitors, mostly Norwegian, visit Spitsbergen on these night trips.

Independent visits, special arrangements

The independent visitors represent perhaps 5% of the 22,000 tourists who come to Spitsbergen annually. Most come for a short stay (see above). Others come as crew on private yachts or with specialist groups or clubs with ambitious aims of long-distance paddling, ice- or rock-climbing. Such activities are not offered as package tours.

Anyone travelling on his own for the first time in Spitsbergen should be well prepared and equipped. He should not establish a set or unchangeable tour:

conditions here are difficult for Europeans to imagine. Familiarize yourself first with the countryside around Longyearbyen and only then attempt a longer tour, so you pay your dues as a novice somewhere near the settlement and not out in the wilderness.

The main problems facing the independent traveller are the following:

* lack of experience of Arctic conditions (the permafrost, moraines, glacial streams and glaciers).
* lack of infrastructure: with no depots available en route, everything must be carried for the planned length of tour. With a heavy rucksack containing provisions for a week (fuel, food, together about 7kg) in addition to all other equipment, average daily progress of an experienced and fit hiker is unlikely to be more than 12 kilometres per day under the Arctic terrain conditions of Svalbard.
* lack of information about local conditions (state of thaw, height of rivers, mud etc). The 1:100000 maps can only give a rough indication of the terrain. Even experienced hikers will find orienteering time-consuming and difficult in this pathless terrain.
* Insufficient equipment (see *Equipment*, *Weapons*).
* Determining how much food and supplies to bring. Specialist food supplies for tours, such as dehydrated meals and many convenience foods, are only occasionally available here. Anyone planning a tour must therefore calculate exactly what will be needed for a demanding tour and bring all these foods with him.

With its lack of infrastructure and its demand for specialist equipment and Arctic experience, Spitsbergen is not the ideal destination for independent travellers wishing to explore the country. Unspoiled nordic wilderness can be experienced at far less effort and cost in other countries. Travellers who reject package tours out of principle should consider whether some other northern destination might not be more suitable for them.

There is however a compromise whereby special arrangements can be made for an individual or special groups by a tour operator. I repeatedly get requests of this type; costs depend on the number of individuals and the kind of tour they wish to have arranged for them.

Unsuitable ways of travelling

Having had so many curious requests about travel in Spitsbergen it seemed relevant to add my comments below.

* Travelling by car, camper, motor-bike or bicycle. There is no car ferry, and the maximum distance that can be travelled is about 24km, still in Longyearbyen. No roads link the settlements. Loose scree, large muddy areas, etc., make the terrain unsuitable for mountain bikes which in addition easily damage the scarce Arctic vegetation.
* Off-road tours. Any motorized traffic is forbidden when there is any risk of damage to plant life.
* Hikes from cabin to cabin. There is no network of trails or supply depots, no cabins for hikers.
* Spitsbergen in three days. It cannot be done. Even in a good year sailing around the main island takes a full week. The coastal vessels only operate on a charter basis. Helicopters may not land in National Parks.

Trekking tours give a taste of real wilderness (Fridtjov glacier).

ADDITIONAL TIPS FOR SPECIAL GROUPS

Alpinists

Occasionally expeditions seeking a challenge visit the islands. The north-west with its igneous rocks and tertiary folding is the best area to tackle walls, ridges and peaks. The experienced ice-climber finds ample opportunities in the spring for glacier treks at a time when old crevasses are generally still filled with drift snow. Helicopters are the only means of transport to these remote areas except in the summer when ships can be chartered. All expedition details should be left with the Governor in case any rescue operation might be necessary.

Journalists

Journalist interest in Spitsbergen has increased over the years. They too should remember that there is no infrastructure and that transport is expensive. The first source of information is the Governor's office, though political questions should be addressed to the ministries in Oslo.

Frequently, journalists unrealistically expect the name of their newspaper or TV company to be a passport for free transport around the islands. This is not the case. A number of projects start ambitiously and end up as a standard Spitsbergen feature from on board a cruise ship when it is realised how difficult it is to get off the beaten track. In my capacity as consultant and logistic adviser for journalists I am always pleased to be involved with projects that aim for something more ambitious.

However, these all require good preparation, sufficient money, and above all enough time in Spitsbergen.

Kayakers and other paddlers

Though at first sight the terrain looks promising, these islands are not well suited for small canoes. Equipment must be of top quality. The Klepper Aerius 1 Expedition kayak or Nautiraid or a one-seater eskimo kayak are recommended (all advanced models used in many military commando units). Additional stern steering equipment is necessary as well as reserve paddles, water-proof rifle holder, integral compass, life-line, survival suits and water-proof storage bags. Tents and camping equipment must also be robust.

Considerable experience and careful planning are essential. Weather conditions change rapidly, making calculations of time extremely difficult. Wind is a constant problem, sometimes blowing drift ice on shore and trapping small canoes or whipping up the seas so that a safe haven cannot be reached. Long stretches of the coast are steep cliffs or glacier fronts which do not even allow emergency landings. Paddling in a survival suit is no pleasure but there is no alternative. Despite these hazards there have been some remarkable achievements by paddlers in recent years.

Streams and rivers are unsuitable, they are short lived and fast flowing.

Private planes

A few private planes land each year from Tromsø, Alta or Banak in northern Norway. Landing fees are high in

Norway and the purchase of a weekly pass, available from any major Norwegian airport, reduces costs. Apart from Longyearbyen there are two other private airstrips, one at Ny Ålesund and the other at Sveagruva . These last two are only for internal traffic. Kerosene should be ordered at least three months in advance.

The radio and weather stations, Bjørnøya Radio on Bear Island and Isfjord Radio at the entrance of Isfjord, are also equipped with radio navigation beacons. Instrument flight equipment is necessary for flights to the islands due to frequent low cloud cover. On approaching the archipelago it is advisable to contact Bjørnøya Radio half way for up to date weather information on Spitsbergen. The Longyearbyen tower receives detailed satellite pictures every few hours. If there is doubt about safe landing it is then not too late to return to the mainland to await better conditions. For navigation the ICAO 1:500,000 map sheets cover the Norwegian mainland and the 1:1,000,000 the Arctic/Svalbard. Within the archipelago the four topographical sheets 1:500,000 are necessary though not entirely reliable as glaciers retreating and developing alter the landscape.

For all Arctic flights complete emergency equipment is, of course, necessary.

Private yachts

About 20-30 yachts visit Spitsbergen each year. Nautical and geographic information is available in the publication *Arctic pilot: Svalbard-Jan Mayen*, Volume 7 edited by the Norsk Sjokartsverk. Experienced sailors who would be interested in joining a private yacht may contact me. I am sometimes asked by owners if I know of crew. Boats need to be steel-hulled and well equipped with radio, radar and echo-sounding equipment. August is the best month, when pack ice has generally retreated and the midnight sun still shines. All repair work will have to be done on board and sufficient supplies carried. A rifle would have to be carried in case of dangerous encounters with a polar bear. Local rules of course must be adhered to and information on national parks and reserves sought before the start of the trip. At both Longyearbyen and Ny Ålesund fresh-water and diesel are available.

Your presence in Spitsbergen waters must be announced via Bjørnøya radio or Isfjord radio.

Skiing tours

Skiing tours require excellent equipment. Conditions are not ideal here, often there is little snow and deep drifts, though the glaciers offer the best possibilities for the very experienced. In many cases snow-shoes may be preferable. Special caution is necessary across fjord ice which locally may be unreliable even in mid-winter and can be broken up by wind within a few days (in Isfjord also by ice-breakers!), thus possibly trapping you on the other side.

EQUIPMENT, WHAT TO BRING

Trekkers are expected to bring all the requisite equipment (including provisions) for their stay away from the settlements. Those travelling with an organised group will have some equipment (tents, cooking utensils) provided and the guides carry fire-arms. Individuals must make sure they have the best quality clothing. Independent travellers must bring all their equipment with them (tents, cooking utensils, fire-arms, signal pistol, etc). The following section offers a rough guide.

The Norwegian administration insists that you bring suitable equipment and may prevent tourists from setting off on trips for which they seem inadequately equipped.

The following equipment is essential:

* Warm wind-breaking clothing for summer and winter.
* Bivouac supplies with sufficient reserves for possible drops in temperature.
* A first-aid kit.
* An emergency signal apparatus.
* The right kind of gun (large calibre).
* For sea trips survival suits are of utmost necessity.

The observations which follow are about pieces of equipment which are important or of specific interest for Spitsbergen. It is not a complete list. When shopping for this type of gear go to a specialist outdoor equipment shop where you can get expert advice. New designs are constantly being introduced by the leading manufacturers.

Tent

The main criterion for a tent in Spitsbergen is wind stability. This means it should be easy to set up, of rugged, high quality construction, and should have a fly sheet which reaches to the ground where it can be fastened. Models with open fly sheets offer the wind an excellent grip, do not protect sufficiently against rain, and above all do not offer the possibility of storing equipment in the bell ends.

The best tents are tunnel-type models which offer the minimum of wind-resistance.

An alternative is a high quality ridge tent with fly sheets that reach to the ground on all sides. In favourable conditions the fly sheet can be used on its own creating more living space and making the tent very light. Ventilation can be regulated better in ridge tents. Phoenix (G.B.) make a very rugged storm-proof tent *Phortress*. The end poles are an upside down V-shape which, although making the tent heavier and less spacious, give excellent stability. The steeper tent sides let rain and snow slip down more easily.

Cupola or dome tents are less suitable. There is little storage space and setting them up in high winds tests the patience.

Pyramid tents are ideal as a base at a camp site. I use one (height 2.6m, diameter 4m) with groups. Though less wind-stable five or six people can live in it. In bad weather it provides a good sheltered room for a larger group to sit together. I also use this model as a work base when I set up field camps for scientific expeditions.

Because of the problem of condensation in Spitsbergen it is important to have good ventilation by having a sufficient distance between the inner and outer sheets. With some domed tents and especially with nylon ones, which expand when wet, the wind can easily push the outer sheet against the inner one and make it wet inside.

It is a good idea to bring the usual aluminum V-shaped tent-pegs, as well as a few of the somewhat larger T-shaped plastic pegs which hold better in soft earth and do not cut through the guy ropes when windy. In addition extra guy ropes are helpful for increasing the tent's stability.

Backpack

Contrary to the general trend, I recommend external frame backpacks for Spitsbergen. For longer tours when you have a lot of equipment or unwieldy articles (a gun, folding boat or dinghy, large containers etc) they make a better choice than a back pack with an inner frame because of the many ways you can pack them and their durability. Inner frame backpacks are appropriate for shorter tours or when you need greater mobility (climbing, difficult skiing tours). The range of high quality models with an outer frame is limited in Europe. In addition to the Swedish makers Fjällräven and Hagløfs the Norwegian Bergans and Norrøna are robust and reliable. The newer frames made of plastic such as Lowe (Holoflex-System) have a flexible frame with hip and shoulder belts which can be easily adjusted to different length backs. Whether they prove themselves in practice remains to be seen; they are very expensive.

Internal frame backpacks should be as large as possible so that everything can be packed away inside.

Whether you decide on an internal or external frame, the backpack should be well and truly tested before you set off on your trip. I know one case of a visitor to Spitsbergen who bought an expensive internal frame backpack. He tested the product at home on a day's hike with about 20kg in it, then started off on a longer tour in Spitsbergen with almost 40kg. The backpack was unwieldy when hung with external packages and proved to be so unsuitable that he was forced to leave the tour. Besides the fact that such a heavy load is hardly ever necessary, it is also beyond the range of an internal frame backpack.

On my longer guided and base supported treks of 2-3 weeks I recommend a minimum sized internal frame model of 75 litres or an external frame model. There is no need to exceed 25kg on these tours; the rifle is the guide's problem. If you travel on your own then an external frame model is the safest way of carrying the rifle, strapped to the outside and readily available in an emergency.

A lighter smaller backpack for day trips is a handy accessory.

Sleeping Bag

Since days or even weeks pass without spending a night in a warm shelter, your sleeping bag is also an item where quality must not be sacrificed.

I find that artificial fibre filled sleeping bags are the best for summer excursions. Down can supply the necessary warmth provided it is dry, but becomes very heavy when wet and dries out slowly (however, down sleeping bags can be waterproofed with TX.10, made by Nikwax). The disadvantage of the artificial fibre is its relative weight compared to its insulation. I spent the last few summers using a new model, the *Spitsbergen*, marketed in Britain by Karrimor, which is filled with a fistulous fibre: *Quallofill*. Although it only weighs about 2kg I was able to sleep well in it dressed in normal underwear, even though it was -4°C in the tent. Other companies offer similar models which provide comparable warmth.

You need to be prepared for temperatures below -5°C in the tent and should, in the interest of getting a good night's sleep, look for sleeping bags which manufacturers describe as being suitable for temperatures from -15 to 20°. The prices for sleeping bags with artificial filling of this quality are usually between £100-£130.

There are some cases in which down is better, on long glacier tours at higher altitudes, for instance, or during the winter when temperatures above freezing, even inside the tent, are the exception and moisture is therefore not a problem.

Apart from a sleeping bag you must have some form of protection against the cold ground. I find a good foam mat 12-15mm thick to be the best solution. The single foam cells must be closed so that water is not absorbed even if the mat is damaged. In contrast to an air mat, which is almost twice as heavy, a foam mat can be placed under the tent as protection from the ground, can be rolled around the tent or sleeping bag as protection when travelling, or used as a seat next to the fire, since sparks from the fire will not damage it.

Stove

After disappointments with two different gas stoves I have had good experiences with my Trangia — a methylated spirit stove with a specially adapted burner for winter conditions. At temperatures around freezing point it lights well, and burns well without becoming too hot to touch. Methyl burners are the most popular during the summer, but I would not assert that they are the best under all conditions. I have a personal preference for them because they are almost unbreakable and tent fires are unlikely to occur (as long as you do not refill a cooker while it is still burning). They use more fuel than other stoves but I am willing to carry this extra weight in exchange for reliability.

If you don't mind the more extensive care which a petrol or oil burner requires you may prefer one of these more thrifty appliances. Methylated spirits, petrol (but perhaps not lead-free) and oil are all available in Longyearbyen.

Water Container

I have had good luck with a sturdy, simple bucket-shaped water bag which, when filled, stands up by itself (since flat ground is unusual, it is a good idea to put the bag between a couple of stones to keep it from spilling).

There is certainly enough water in Spitsbergen, but not always close to an otherwise suitable camping spot. The nearest stream may be full of safe but unappetising glacial sediment, so be prepared with a reasonable sized container to reduce the chore of water carrying.

Containers with taps are not satisfactory. Trying to fill them from a stream is exhausting and getting water out of them is only easy when you can hang them up — a difficulty in Spitsbergen where there are no trees or bushes.

With the right equipment, camping is possible in all conditions.

Clothing

The well known layering principle also applies here — a
lot of thin layers are better than a few thick articles. The
clothing should protect above all against wind chill,
without impeding sweat evaporation. You should carry
enough spare clothing with you to change into after an
unplanned stream bath.

An anorak should be the outermost layer, as
impermeable to wind as possible and with a wind-tight
fastening around the hips, hood, hands and front
closures. It should reach down over the hips. My
preference is for anoraks with full length two way zippers
and an extra closure of press-fasteners, since they permit
better temperature control.

A high quality anorak, of Gore-Tex or something
similar, for protection against the wet is certainly a good
idea and makes other rain-wear superfluous. Recently I
have used an unlined Gore-Tex anorak under which I
can put a fleece jacket if really necessary. A good
quality, durable anorak which wears well has its price,
however.

I find thick military parkas are less suitable since they
are heavy, especially when wet, and dry slowly. Thick
down jackets are only partially useful in the summer:
when carrying a heavy pack in one you sweat; once you
take it off you will be too cold. Occasionally a warm
down jacket can be comfortable in camp during a
summer tour.

Army surplus trousers are generally inexpensive and
wear well, but have the disadvantage of drying slowly.
Skin-tight trousers restrict movement and a thin warming
layer between skin and material is important.

Some people use Gore-Tex hiking trousers. In addition to protecting against rain some hikers have used them for wading through streams. If you fasten the bottoms of the waterproofs to your boots with a strong elastic band you can make a few careful short steps through deep water without it rushing into your boots. This applies to any pair of good waterproof trousers.

Long underwear should also be part of your luggage for a summer visit. They should only be worn on the few really cold days since you'll generate enough warmth from walking. Warm underwear is pleasant to wear in camp and at night.

Polar fleece is a very practical material, sturdy and not sensitive to moisture. It dries quickly, holds warmth well and most people find it pleasant to wear. In addition to the more common fleece jackets and trousers there are also fleece socks. They are an especially good idea for canoeists as part of their water-proof clothing, and practical for hikers as reserve clothing. In addition to resistance to wear and tear they keep your feet warm (even when they are wet, important when making long hikes in rubber boots) and dry quickly. Beware how you experiment with drying them though, they do not like heat.

Special attention should be given to footwear since feet get tired on long hikes. In addition to the right shoes you should wear high quality hiking socks, especially when wearing rubber boots, since they protect the feet and absorb much of the moisture. All footwear, including socks, should be thoroughly tried out at home to make certain it suits you before you purchase the requisite number of pairs.

Clothing does not dry well in cold damp weather. Under these conditions it is most practical to let damp clothes dry on you, covering yourself up with a sleeping bag to avoid getting too cold. The drying process is accelerated if moisture can evaporate unhindered (by leaving the zipper of the sleeping bag open at the bottom, for instance), but can still take hours.

The choice of clothing is more complicated for those travelling by boat. Good protection is needed against not only the water, but also the wind. Fingers are especially difficult to protect without hindering paddling. On warm windless days you can find yourself sweating under the protective clothing. Wet suits which are thick enough are not comfortable, may chafe your skin, and are not always warm enough in the wind, especially when dry.

The sauna effect caused by dry suits can be reduced by materials which breathe as well as by moisture absorbent underwear. These models are costly, but recommended for longer tours. High quality survival suits are recommended by the authorities. These incorporate shoes, gloves and a hood and ensure survival for nine hours even in ice-cold water. In the future these may become obligatory. Irrespective of this, the individual would be well advised to wear a suit of this kind. The sudden change in the sea can turn any trip into a real risk, even if the boat is sea worthy, especially if landing is made impossible by steep shores, breakers, glacier fronts or shallows.

Footwear

For day trips or trekking tours of just a few days good rubber hiking boots are perfectly acceptable. On long demanding tours I prefer heavy plastic mountaineering boots. Anyone who is used to mountain boots usually reads with disbelief that you can hike comfortably in rubber boots. I had to be converted during an earlier trip in Lapland. Quite impractical, of course, are inexpensive Wellington boots. The rubber boots should reach almost to the knee (40cm high) for crossing glacier streams. Models that can be unrolled up to the thigh are especially useful if they are light and flexible. Fishermen's boots are too heavy for hiking.

Care must be taken in buying boots. They must be really comfortable and give adequate support to the foot in order to avoid orthopaedic complications on longer tours. If necessary you can try an insole. Also important is a good tread and a pair that will stand up to sharp stones.

Light so-called trekking shoes, a cross between trainers and mountaineering boots, are, in my view, generally unsuitable for long trekking. The demands of the terrain are too much for them. Either the sides of the shoes are not high enough or they do not offer enough protection and rigidity. I find such shoes only useful for day trips when they can be dried overnight in a warm place.

Except for wading through streams, my favourite footwear are heavy plastic mountaineering boots for long treks. The Austrian model *Koflach Ultra* or the Italian *Asolo AFS 102* are both recommended. They both have a well padded separate inner shoe with a thin sole. They are warm, protect feet from blisters and are comfortable, especially when carrying a heavy rucksack. The light inner shoes can be worn on their own in camp. The outer shoes are plastic with laces and are good protection against loose scree or for walking across stony glacier stream beds. They allow a firm step on hard snow slopes and crampons can easily be fixed to them. More importantly for Svalbard they are waterproof, useful on the often wet terrain and for crossing shallow streams. For deeper streams rubber boots are needed if you wish to keep your feet dry. However, as a last resort in deep water the inner shoes can be removed from the plastic boots and replaced dry on the other side of the stream once the outer boot has been emptied and the feet dried. As you should never cross the often violent glacier streams bare-footed this method will save you from having to carry an extra pair of shoes for these occasional crossings.

I recommend that shoes are properly tested as realistically as possible in advance. Years ago I bought a pair of rubber hiking boots, one of which proved to be unsound after just a few steps because of a manufacturing flaw. This is the sort of thing to be discovered at home, and not in Spitsbergen. Equally it is a good idea to know where the shoe rubs so that blisters can be prevented.

Climbing Accessories

Climbing accessories can prove useful even for those who plan to avoid glaciers. On excursions in Spitsbergen you often have to cross small ice or snow fields on which shoes without crampons can only give unsteady footing. Crampons require practice and the right bindings and spike covers so that you can store them without damaging other things.

Rain Gear

Since it seldom rains hard for any length of time and normal rain suits create a sauna effect, a poncho or a light but rugged Gore-Tex suit seems to me to be the most suitable rain wear for Spitsbergen. Occasionally, when there is a strong wind, a poncho has disadvantages. Squeezing an external frame backpack under a poncho with closed sides is often impossible, even with a mountaineer's poncho with its special gusset at the back. I prefer large ponchos which can be closed at the sides with a row of press fasteners. Although they do not fit tightly, most backpacks fit underneath and the press fasteners allow a reasonable fit and ventilation from the sides. When the rain stops it can be draped over your backpack and shoulders so that it protects but does not create unnecessary condensation problems. Very light models are available which fold easily.

Heavy military ponchos bought new or second hand (hold it up to the light to check for holes) are also practical. They are durable and can be used as a ground sheet or emergency bivouac.

I find it better, on the rare occasions when underway in strong rain and wind, to protect my backpack with a plastic tarpaulin. Tie it down securely. I have seen even elastic sided covers blow off.

Tools

You should always include a pocketknife, and a few oddments (sewing kit, insulating tape, wire, rope, patches of leather and cloth, adhesive) in your equipment to make repairs to your kit during the trip. For tours along the coast, an axe for log splitting can be useful especially if you are in a group and can divide up the extra weight.

Photography

One should be prepared for poor light conditions, since in summer the sun is quite low. Although it remains above the horizon at night, the light is often insufficient for capturing moving animals. The islands offer many opportunities to use a telephoto lens, both for landscape and wildlife pictures. A tripod is necessary in weak light or a fast film speed.

My favourite combination is Kodachrome 25 or 64 for landscapes and Kodachrome 200 Ektachrome 200 for moving subjects. With cloudy sky — a frequent situation — Ektachrome 50 or Ektachrome 100 may be better for landscape because they document fine differences in colour better than Kodachrome. This choice is a question of taste since other companies make films which emphasize different colours, and which react differently in the Arctic than at lower latitudes. Bring enough film with you since the price of film in Spitsbergen is about twice that in Europe.

Skylight and ultra violet filters are recommended. As you will probably want to take some animal pictures, a strong telephoto lens — 300mm or a 500mm mirror lens — is very desirable, even for landscapes due to the often extremely clear air that allows shots of very distant subjects. Tie the lens cap on since you cannot get a replacement here.

My experiences in Spitsbergen have taught me to prize my mechanical single lens reflex camera even more since its reliability is only slightly dependent on batteries — a plus when you are on an excursion where the camera will be cold for weeks. Electronic cameras use up batteries very quickly if they are not warmed before every use.

The mechanical camera seemed even more fortuitous when on one tour the battery cover fell off and I lost the batteries in my old Canon FT QL. With the help of a separate hand-held light meter I could still use the camera, whereas most small modern cameras are nothing more than ballast in your backpack without batteries.

I keep my photographic equipment handy on land tours in two hip bags with leather strengthened straps (to prevent fraying) lashed to a separate hip belt.

Equipment tips

In addition, a British tour operator suggests an eye mask for sleeping. To keep your feet warm wear a plastic bag between your first layer of thin socks and second layer of thick ones. This way perspiration stays within the thin socks, which you will change every day and the thick socks and shoes keep dry and warm. Insulation and comfort are increased. Finally, knee high gaiters may be preferred over rubber boots for stream crossings.

Even on a short-stay programme, visitors can experience the pathless wilderness near a settlement.

FIREARMS

Even if there was nothing new for a Lapland expert in the equipment description above, information about guns will only be 'old hat' for a very small number of those who buy this book. This is one of the ways in which Spitsbergen is significantly different from other wilderness areas in Europe. Anyone travelling with a package tour does not need to worry about a gun. This section is intended as advice for those few who are planning an independent trip.

Suitable Weapons

A firearm for Spitsbergen must be sturdy, reliable, of sufficiently large calibre and big cartridge magazine. In the summer of 1987 a scientist only succeeded in driving away a bear after firing five warning shots.

If the gun is only needed for the trip to Spitsbergen look for a used .308 Winchester or 8mm or 30-06 carbine which takes five cartridges in its magazine. Carbines are generally very reliable weapons but the cheaper ones may well have a long history behind them.

I have already heard two stories in Spitsbergen where the repeat did not function properly on used weapons, rendering them of little use. A second shot should always be available, whether as warning to drive the animal away, or to follow up a poor hit. Carbines are available from about £200 second hand to about £500 new.

The disadvantage of the carbine is the limited number of shots, and that reloading takes precious time when faced by an attacking polar bear (with speeds up to 60km per hour). In this instance a reliable semi-automatic rifle is considerably better. With these loading is automatic so you only have to concentrate on aiming your next shot. They are seldom available used, but are offered by a variety of manufacturers.

To my knowledge, among semi-automatic weapons used for self-defence, the model Petra produced by the Finnish manufacturer Valmet, which I use myself, is one of the best. Its size is manageable, the gun-sight fast, and it is as sturdy as the famous Russian Kalashnikov of which it is a copy. These weapons cost around £450 new. Their large magazine capacity (up to nine cartridges) increases your security in an encounter with a polar bear. The animal can be frightened off first with a few warning shots, whereas with a carbine you may begin to panic after firing the second warning shot and may then see no other choice but to shoot the bear as you run out of ammunition in the magazine.

Semi-automatics are less suitable for use in the winter, since when it gets very cold the release mechanism can freeze. In general, guns should be left out in the cold so that water doesn't condense in them which could freeze or rust later.

In addition to these most common weapons, there are a few others suitable for self-defence against polar bears. The calibre must be .308 Winchester or larger.

An alternative to the rifle is the pump-action shotgun loaded with pellets which can also be used to shoot signal cartridges, although they do not achieve the same effect as a larger signal pistol (4 calibre). Since using a pump-action shotgun and pellets is so different from using a rifle you should have practice before leaving. There is no ammunition available for them in Spitsbergen, although there is for common calibre rifles.

All of the weapons described are intended for quick and secure self-defence and are less suitable for precision sporting shooting. In Norway semi-automatics with more than two shots are prohibited in Norway for hunting. These weapons are only useful for self-defence against polar bears. Loaded guns may not be carried in the settlements.

Unsuitable Weapons

These include shot guns: shot is intended for smaller prey. Only pump-action shotguns loaded with several cartridges can be an adequate weapon against a bear, as there is the possibility of firing several warning shots before taking a direct shot.

Similarly unsuitable are pistols and revolvers which will only stop an animal weighing 500kg or more if you hit the right place. Even the heaviest .44 Magnum has only half the velocity of a .308 cartridge but these uncommon weapons are more expensive than many large calibre guns and require a strong hand because of the heavy recoil. Furthermore, they are illegal for self-defence in Spitsbergen.

Incidentally, even the best gun is useless if kept tightly secured in the rucksack. There is no point in carrying a gun if you cannot reach it quickly in an emergency.

Training

If proper training has not been undertaken then carrying a weapon is only of psychological use (self-deception) or of value as endurance training since you are lugging around a few extra kilos.

In an emergency an inexperienced person has only a slim chance of using a weapon correctly and effectively. In the heat of the moment he will probably shoot too soon, before the situation has become an emergency, and may kill one of these mighty animals unnecessarily.

Anyone travelling to Spitsbergen should be familiar with his weapon; to do this you must practice. In Great Britain the opportunities are scarce; most ranges are on Ministry land. (In order to purchase any large calibre weapon in Britain a fire-arm permit must be obtained from the police.)

Warning and Distress Signals

In addition to radios (see A Guide from A to Z) star shells are a good way of attracting helicopter attention. Because of the remoteness of the countryside the star shell should be visible from as far away as possible. A large signal pistol (4 calibre, 27mm) as used by the police and armed forces is ideal for this purpose. Its shots climb 300 metres high and can be seen from far away. You may, however, need a weapons permit to buy one.

Distress signals can also be used to drive away a polar bear, especially if it is the type which causes a strong flash of light and a loud noise. Especially good are the thunderflash hand grenades. (See section on polar bears for their use.)

The weapon used for defence should always be kept ready to fire since explosives do not always make an impression on a bear.

Probably the most reliable signal apparatus is the SARSAT system or emergency beacons. It is not cheap, however. About the size of a hand radio, it emits a signal which is picked up and transmitted by satellite. It was in this way that a rescue team was able to quickly reach a helicopter which had crashed in the north of Spitsbergen. At present, however, they are only allowed on boats and aircraft.

DETAILED INFORMATION A-Z

This chapter introduces a selection of local services and topics of interest to visitors. Those which are in Longyearbyen are numbered and can be located on the town map.

Accommodation

Modest tourist accommodation is available in Longyearbyen in renovated company buildings. The 1991 price for a single room in Nybyen (10) is 485.-nkr (£44/$88 approx.), including breakfast. Each accommodation block has a lounge, kitchen and bathroom on its two floors. *Funken* in Haugen (10) offers a higher standard, single rooms cost from 630.-nkr to 920.-nkr for a suite with a bath. The reception hall (9), and breakfast room is in Nybyen where bicycles can be rented. Maps, books and postcards are also available. Transport by helicopter and bookings for accommodation in Barentsburg or Pyramiden can be made here or at the office building, (Reisebyrå, 18). In

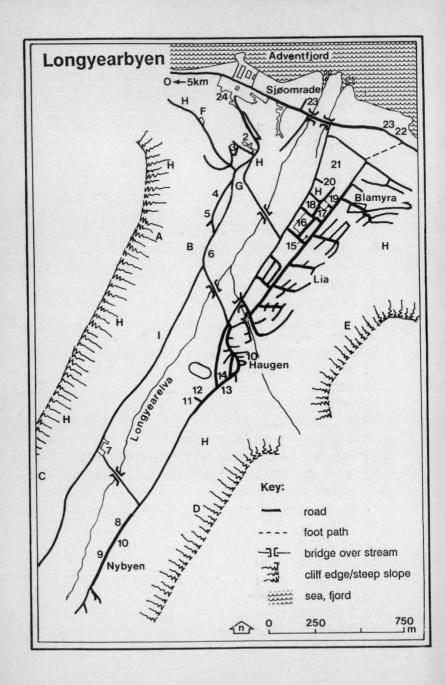

Longyearbyen
Places of interest
A   Old funicular junction road to airport and campsite
B   Remains of pre-war Longyearbyen
C   Old Mine 1
D   Old Graveyard
E   New Mine 1
F   New Mine 2
G   Old Mine 2
0   Road to airport, camp-site, coalport, Mine 3
1   Pier
2   Governor, Police, registration of tours
3   Telecommunications office
4   Church, Community Hall
5   Kindergarten
6   Svalbard Museum
7   'Huset': Restaurant, Kiosk, Cinema
8   Svalbardbutikken (general store). See also 15
9   Reception, bicycle hire
10 Accommodation buildings
11 School
12 Swimming pool
13 Hospital (until 1992)
14 SNSK office building
15 Planned new Svalbardbutikken (due 1996)
16 'Lompen': library, fresh food shop, Cafeteria 'Kafe Busen'
17 Bank, Post Office
18 Office building
19 Youth club
20 New hospital (1992)
21 Planned hotel (about 1993)
22 Yamaha, Polaris, Avis
23 Skinnboden
24 Provianten food shop

1990, a night in a double room in Barentsburg or Pyramiden was offered for 310.-nkr per person without breakfast. A planned, high standard, 60 room hotel (21) with cinema, restaurant and bar has been postponed and is unlikely to be available before 1993.

See also *Restaurants*.

There are no hostels or cabins for tourists outside the settlements; the few scattered cabins are for scientists, special permission for their hire can be obtained from the *Sysselmann* (see below), this facility is not available to tourists. In cases of extreme emergency they could be used but generally their occupation is not allowed.

Bank (17)

The Svalbard Sparebank is situated in the same dark brown building as the Post Office. Open Monday to Friday 10.00-16.00 (Thursday 10.00-18.00). It is advisable to bring travellers' cheques rather than cash as, like all banks in Norway, the bank rates are high and the exchange rate unfavourable. Telephone orders for money transfer from your own bank is also possible (but fees are high). There is no on-line information on the International Stock Exchange.

Bicycle Rental

Since 1989 good bicycles can be rented in Longyearbyen at the reception hall (9) of the accommodation block, Nybyen. The rate in 1989 was 85.-nkr per day with special reduced rates for longer periods.

Cabins see *Accommodation*

Cafeteria and Canteen see *Restaurant*

Campsites

A designated campsite is provided on Hotelneset, about 5km from the centre of Longyearbyen. Camping elsewhere in the town or within 7km is not permitted as this is private land belonging to the coal company. The campsite was chosen and a service building installed in 1985 (enlarged in 1988). The charge is 60.-nkr per person per night (1990), a massive rise from 15.-nkr which was charged up to 1987. Unfortunately, it is hardly possible for the newcomer to avoid this campsite, even if you are not interested in its facilities, because it is difficult to start immediately from the airport on a tour. With the ban on camping in a large area around Longyearbyen, the campsite has a monopoly. However, when returning from an arduous tour it is wonderful to have the possibility of a hot shower (coin-operated, each token costs 5.-nkr, lasting for about two minutes), to find washing machines (washing fee 10.-nkr) and tumble driers and to eat in a warm room. As the room has a limited capacity, do not block the few tables once you have finished your meal but make way for others. Clean up your rubbish from the tables and floor before leaving! Respect the rule "shoes off inside the building" — coal dust around the campsite is difficult for the supervisor to clean. Maps of the surroundings of Longyearbyen, and postcards etc. are sometimes for sale, also a few books and paraffin. Tokens are also for sale at 5.-nkr to operate the showers. One token is sufficient for hot water for a quick shower. Don't be antisocial and horde these tokens as there is a shortage and you will block the shower's use by others if there are no more available.

After using the showers and wash basins, clean up after yourself; no one else wants to get wet socks.

On the outside of the building there are several heated toilet cabins which are accessible during the summer season, even when the service building is locked. There is also a cold water tap and hose, useful for cleaning equipment. Like most buildings in Longyearbyen the block is raised on poles, designed to prevent heat from the building from melting the permafrost. This creates a well ventilated space where equipment can be stored (at your own risk). It should be well packed against the coal dust.

During the season (mid-June until end of August) there are up to 50 tents on the site simultaneously (though some of them are there permanently, occasionally used by tour operators for their groups). Though this sounds a lot there is space for several times more. The service building then gets quite crowded. During the last few seasons the attendant has registered around 1,400 overnight stays in the 9-10 weeks that the building is open. During the rest of the year the site is almost deserted and the only facilities then are a primitive wooden toilet and a stream or melted snow for water. Camping is free then, but it requires a certain immunity against cold and perfect equipment to withstand the conditions on this wind-beaten strand. Therefore about 95% of camping tourism is concentrated in the ten summer weeks. Even in summer the wind-swept camp site is an excellent place to test how storm-proof your tent is! Furthermore, with the wind coming from the south-east it brings fine coal dust from the nearby storage piles. However, the campsite offers a marvellous view across the Isfjord with the impressive glaciers on its northern side.

From the campsite it is about 5km to the town following the road that leads from the airport. At the junction close to the coal depot turn right and use the upper road behind the coal silos. This road, closed to motor traffic, allows a better view across the shore. If you plan to spend a reasonable length of time at the campsite a bicycle can be rented from the reception hall (9).

Ny Ålesund has a campsite (northernmost in the world) (see page 110) but there are no other designated campsites. When setting up camp elsewhere respect the residents' privacy and leave no trace of your stay.

See also *Bicycle* and *Shopping*.

Car rental

Cars can be rented in the new service building of SNSK (18) and from the Yamaha dealer (22) and from the AVIS representation. Prices start somewhere (1990) around 400.-nkr/day or 2100.-nkr/week or 6000.-nkr/month for a Subary Justy. Other car models for rent are, for instance, Toyota Carina Combi, Toyota Tercel, Toyota Corolla, Subary Legacy or Mercedes. A current international driver's licence is required. There are only 22kms of road outside Longyearbyen from Mine 7 in Adventdalen to the entrance of Bjorndalen. There are occasional traffic controls in Longyearbyen, generally for breathalysing.

See also *Internal Traffic*, *Bicycle*.

Cinema

At least one film is shown per week in Longyearbyen at *Huset* (7), on Sundays usually at 19.00. They are generally in English with Norwegian subtitles. When the new hotel (21) is complete there is also a planned

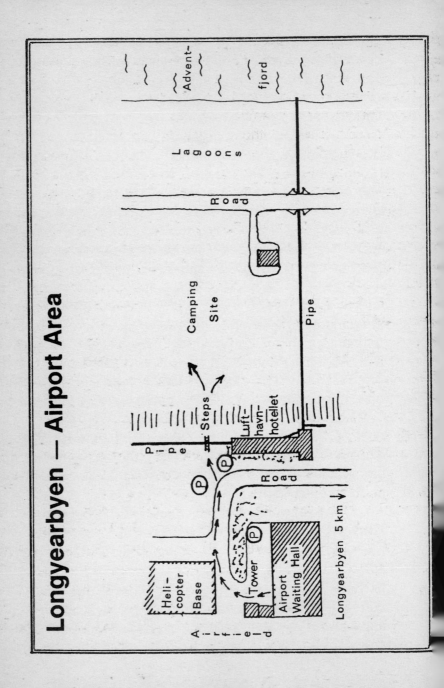

Longyearbyen — Airport Area

new hotel (21) is complete there is also a planned cinema on the site. Barentsburg has several showings per week, but in Russian.

Credit cards
Only a few credit cards are accepted, and not everywhere in the Norwegian settlements (none in Barentsburg and Pyramiden). Most common are VISA and American Express, occasionally Eurocard.

Cultural monuments
As relatively little is known about the history of Svalbard and many parts of the country are rarely visited it is not uncommon to come across historical remains. When I was on a trekking tour recently I found an old claim sign in Grondalen. The Arctic climate is a good preserver of remnants of human activity. Should you make such a find, leave the site untouched and inform the Governor's office on return. There is an official (Kulturvernkonsulent) concerned with cultural monuments.

All human traces prior to 1900 are protected by law on Svalbard and Jan Mayen and must not be destroyed, excavated, moved or altered in any way. Any inscribed stones, graves, land claims etc of a more recent date should be left untouched.

Currency
As Svalbard is part of Norway the currency used is the Norwegian crown (norske kroner, nkr in Norwegian or NOK the international abbreviation). The former internal currency of the coal company in Longyearbyen has been abolished. The availability of goods for Norwegian crowns in the Soviet settlements is uncertain, however

you will almost inevitably be contacted there by locals who try to make a deal with the tourists for western currency.

The Soviet coal company, Turst Arktikugol, has its own internal company money — notes with denominations of 1, 2, 3, 5, 10 and 20 kopecks and bigger ones for 1, 3, 5, 10, etc., roubles. These notes are different from normal Soviet bank notes — a nice souvenir, typical Spitsbergen.

Exchange rates: in October 1990, £1 = 11.25 Norwegian kroner (nkr); $1 = 22.-nkr.

Customs
Svalbard has been a free trade zone since the Svalbard Treaty. There is no Norwegian customs or value added tax, unlike Norway where the VAT is 20%. Other taxes on such items as alcohol, cars, and tobacco which are very high in Norway do not exist on Svalbard so these goods are very cheap by Norwegian standards. However when such goods are imported into Norway naturally national taxes have to be paid. When returning to the Norwegian mainland, tourists must declare goods from Spitsbergen. Police officials at Longyearbyen can check baggage at the airport to avoid delays at Tromsø if you are taking an ongoing flight.

Entry requirements
No visa is necessary for citizens of countries that have signed the Svalbard treaty to visit Svalbard (however a visa may be needed for mainland Norway for the journey to Svalbard and back!). All visitors planning a hiking tour must bring adequate equipment and supplies for the length of their stay (see *Equipment*). Visitors without the necessary equipment risk being denied entry. Presently

(autumn 1990), new more detailed rules for tourists are in preparation, affecting those who want to leave the area of the settlements. These rules probably will require an approval of the planned tour and insurance for search and rescue operations. Tour operators will take care of these requirements on behalf of their clients.

See also *Customs*, *Fire-arms*, *Pets*, *Registration*.

Firearms

Any visitor who travels outside the settlements is expected to carry a suitable gun for self-defence against polar bears. Guides accompanying a tour take care of this.

Suitable guns must be of .308 calibre or larger; revolvers and pistols are not acceptable. All documents pertaining to your weapon, proving ownership and right of use, must be brought with you and presented to the authorities at the Sysselmann's office if requested.

Restrictions on hunting weapons (no more than 2 shot magazine capacity, no slugs) do not apply to those used in self defence.

In settlements weapons must be carried unloaded.

It is advisable either to send fire-arms by freight in advance or to check them as special luggage on your flight. When travelling by land there are delays at every border crossing having to declare weapons and ammunition, especially annoying if travelling by train. Do not be persuaded to cross borders without making a declaration: there might be severe consequences. Sweden expects a transit security fee which was 200 skr. for each weapon in 1987.

See *Equipment* chapter and the section on polar bears in chapter 1.

Fuel

Fuel for stoves (petrol, paraffin) is available at the *materiallager* (a large blue building at the pier) in bottles, sometimes from the campsite attendant, Svalbardbutikk (8, 15) or Yamaha (22). Some types of Camping Gaz cylinders are also available. Fuel for rental cars is available at the petrol station in the sea area. To operate the petrol pumps a special magnetic card is necessary. Contact the counter of materiallager.

Governor see *Sysselmann*

Horse riding

In late summer 1990, seven Icelandic ponies were brought to Longyearbyen and can be rented for sledge or coach trips or riding in town. The stable is on Hotelineset next to the coal storage area.

Hotel see *Accommodation*

Hunting

Details and regulations should be obtained in advance from the Sysselmann. Hunting is only possible outside the national parks, nature reserves and animal sanctuaries. The following lists hunting seasons for each species which should be confirmed at the Governor's office.

Arctic fox (*Polarrev*). 1st November-15th March. Certain lethal traps permitted. Protected on Bear Island.

Bearded seal (*Storkobbe*) and ringed seal (*Ringsel*). All year except 15th March-15th April.

Brunnich's guillemot (*Polarlomvi*), common guillemot (*Lomvi*), fulmar (*Havhest*), little auk (*Alkekonge*), black guillemot (*Teist*), pink-footed goose (*Kortnebbgas*), puffin (*Lunde*) only September and October.

Glaucous gull (*Polarmake*) all year round.

Ptarmigan (*Svalbardrype*) September to March, protected on Bear Island.

During the season all hunting is forbidden on Good Friday, Easter Sunday and between December 24th and 31st. Restricted reindeer hunting is allowed for residents during August and September, not for visitors. Semi-automatics with more than two shots and slug ammunition are forbidden for hunting. Furthermore hunting from ships, aircraft or any motorized vehicle is prohibited in tracking, following or chasing animals.

Internal traffic
There is no regular traffic between settlements: no roads, no buses, flights or ferries. A first attempt of operating a regular ship service between Longyearbyen and Ny Ålesund in 1990 twice a week during the two summer months failed due to insufficient passengers. Transport can be chartered or the traveller has to rely on last minute space becoming available.

Air traffic: There are three (1990) helicopters with commercial licences based in Longyearbyen : 1 Aerospatiale AS-350 with max. 5 passengers, no luggage and max. 1 hour flying), price per flight hour in 1991 probably 9,500.-nkr, and 2 Bell UH-212 with max. 9 passengers (17,000.-nkr/flight hour, priority for the Governor). In addition, there is a Partenavia Spartacus (twin-engined turbo-prop plane) for seven passengers (1990: 10,850.-nkr/flight hour) available, which is, however, restricted to the three landing fields

(Longyearbyen, Sveagruva, Ny Ålesund). Empty return
flights have to be paid, too. As an example, a helicopter
flight from Longyearbyen to Barentsburg or Pyramiden
and back costs (1990) 1,050.-nkr per person (requiring
a minimum of four participants) and takes about 15
minutes in each direction. The Soviet helicopters in
Barentsburg have no commercial licence. In general
internal flights are expensive due to maintenance and
staffing costs.

Sea transport: 6-8 coastal charter vessels with 11-46
cabins are due to operate during the summer months
(June-early September). Booking can be done in
advance through a travel agent or tour operator.
Chartering an 11 berth vessel costs approx. 16,000.-nkr
per day, 46 berth 50,000.-nkr. Occasionally stand-by
places are available on short 3-12 hr. fjord cruises, no
guarantees of course. On longer cruises to Ny Ålesund
for example any available spare berths are made public
in the entrance of the cafeteria (16), the Huset (7) and
office building (18 Reisebyrå). The Sysselmann's vessel
MS Palarsyssel can be chartered for moving large
equipment. It has a solid boom and helicopter pad.
However, of course emergency official duty will have
priority. It is usually in Spitsbergen from May to
December.

Land transport: During the summer, motorized traffic is
only allowed on the few roads as when the land thaws
tracks are permanently left in the ground for years to
come. Three taxis operate in Longyearbyen (in 1989 the
cost was 60.-nkr to the campsite and 110.-nkr from
Longyearbyen to the entrance of Bolterdalen) at least
one is always available at any time. Bicycles and cars

can also be hired. Motor sledges (minimum age 16, requiring a licence) can be hired in the winter (500.- nkr/day). These are of interest particularly in March and April when there is daylight but the ground is still frozen. During the polar night they require considerable experience and skill. At Easter it is hard to find one to hire as so many relatives visit the islands.

Medical services

There is a hospital in Longyearbyen in Haugen (13) with a staff of 18 and dental and physiotherapy treatment available. A new hospital is planned in Lia (20) by 1992 with six beds for general use and one intensive care unit. Barentsburg has a large hospital and ambulance stations are situated in Ny Ålesund, Pyramiden and Sveagruva. Make sure your medical insurance includes Norway.

Museums

Svalbard Museum (6) in Longyearbyen is the best known and certainly worth a visit. It was opened in 1981 when 3,000 visitors were recorded, a figure which has gradually risen to over 9,000 in 1989. Opening times are variable during the summer, but it can be expected to be open every day for a few hours. The night charter flights and cruise ships are catered for on request. Over the years the museum has grown and new exhibits are found outside (B), including a polar bear trap, ancient hunting cabin, fishing boat, sledges etc. The second floor is used as a special exhibition area. The building is the oldest in the town and was previously a stable; the old bakery next door is now incorporated into the museum. A few poles and ruins (B) on the slope above are a reminder of the devastation to the settlement in World War II.

Exhibits cover natural history (geology, fossils, climate, plants and animals) and the settlement (whalers, hunters, trappers) and exploration (expeditions, mining) of Svalbard. A selection of books, maps, brochures, posters, cards etc. are on sale.

Barentsburg's museum is older and has a detailed section on the natural conditions of the islands and Soviet involvement on the archipelago. It is open every day except Mondays. Smaller local collections are in museums in Ny Ålesund and on Bear Island. These mainly deal with local history and are open on request.

If you travel to Spitsbergen via Tromsø don't miss the Polar museum there.

Nature conservation

A free booklet, *Environmental regulations for Svalbard and Jan Mayen*, is issued by the Royal Norwegian Ministry of the Environment and is usually available at the Governor's office (2), airport and campsite. Read the regulations carefully. See also *Rubbish*, *Hunting*, *Internal traffic*, *Cultural monuments*.

Conservation is taken very seriously on Spitsbergen due to the special vulnerability of the Arctic which only recovers slowly from any damage. Caterpillar tracks from 70 years ago are still clearly visible as scars in the thin vegetation and litter remains for decades as reminders of carelessness. The following apply to all of Svalbard:

*   No motorized traffic off the roads unless the ground is entirely frozen.

* Don't damage the vegetation; pitch tents and make fires on bare ground only. Do not dig up plants unnecessarily.
* Take all litter with you. Litter can harm curious animals (ropes, glass splinters, plastic bags, tins etc).
* Do not disturb birds, particularly on their breeding grounds. Leave an area immediately so that eggs are not abandoned or adults unduly distressed by your presence. Loud noises must be avoided which might cause panic amongst the colony. It is forbidden to fire a shot or hoot a ship's horn within a kilometre of nesting cliffs during the breeding season or to fly over such places at an altitude of less than 500m.
* Do not chase wildlife even if it is in order to photograph or study them. They rapidly lose energy. In winter this can be a lethal threat to ptarmigans, reindeer and polar bears. Disturbances can divide young from adults. As recently as 1989 three motor-sledge drivers were fined 8,000.-nkr for separating a female polar bear from her cubs while trying to get sensational photographs.

About half of Svalbard is protected either as national parks or nature reserves; 20 smaller areas are designated sanctuaries.

In view of the special international status of Svalbard where many nations have considerable rights, the definition of such extended protected areas was no easy task.

In addition to the general rules already quoted the following are applicable:

* National Parks: No hunting, collecting of plants or fossils, disturbance or damage to mammals, birds and their nests and eggs. The use of cross country

vehicles at all times and the landing of aircraft, construction (except navigation aids), mining and exploration and fishing (except below a depth of 100m) is forbidden. Exceptions can be made for valid scientific purposes and, of course, the rescue and police services.

* Nature reserves: As for national parks but the additional right to stop all traffic when considered necessary.
* Plant reserves: All damage to vegetation, including the pitching of tents, is forbidden.
* Bird sanctuaries: As for national parks; in addition all human passage is prohibited between 15th April and 15th August.
* Moffen reserve: As for national parks and a restriction of 300m from shore for ships, 500m altitude for aircraft, between 15th May and 15th September. The removal of any skeletal parts, including teeth, is illegal. The island is of particular importance for the small stock of walrus around Svalbard.
* King Karls Land: As for nature reserves, and ships and planes must keep a minimum distance at all times. The area is of special importance for the breeding of polar bears.

A few exceptions to these strict rules are granted to residents. For example motor sledges are allowed on a few defined routes in the national parks and in Ny Friesland and in the immediate areas of the settlements. Dispensation is granted from the protection of all plant life for maintenance work to the settlements (both Longyearbyen and Pyramiden are within plant reserves). However the strict rules have been adhered to at the latest drilling station at Haketangen where everything has been extremely well cleared up, unlike earlier sites such as Berzeliusdalen.

The location of the protected areas can be seen on the following page.

Opening Times

For its size Longyearbyen has an impressive infrastructure. Understandably, there is no need to have extensive opening times for all shops and institutions for such a small population. In summer, during the midnight sun, visitors are surprised by the strange opening times deep in the 'night'.

In general most facilities are open between 10.00-12.00.

Pets

Rabies occurs in Svalbard — but not in mainland Norway. Accordingly, it is illegal to bring animals to Svalbard and from Svalbard to the Norwegian mainland. Exceptions: animals which have been in quarantine in Norway for observation for several weeks and small pets of locals (cage birds, rabbits, etc.).

Police see *Sysselmann*

Post

The main post office is in Longyearbyen (17) together with the bank. Opening times as for the bank plus Saturdays 10.00-12.00. Post office savings books (provided there are reciprocal arrangements with Norway) are a good way of getting Norwegian kroner at a reasonable exchange rate. The postal service is relatively good. Letter boxes are found at the museum,

National Parks
and other protected areas

N.P. = National Park   N.R. = Nature Reserve
      = Plant Reserve

(One Plant Reserve, Ossian Sars in Kongsfjord, is too
small to be marked in this scale)

1-16 = Bird or Walrus Sanctuaries:

1 Sørkapp	9 Fordlandsøyane
2 Dunøyane	10 Hermansenøya
3 Isøyane	11 Kongsfjorden
4 Olsholmen	12 Blomstrandhamna
5 Kap Linné	13 Guissezholmen
6 Boheman	14 Skorpa
7 Gåsøyane	15 Moseøya
8 Plankeholmane	16 Moffen

airport, and Huset (7). There are sub post offices (*brevhus*) at Ny Ålesund, Sveagruva, Isfjord Station, Bjørnøya, and Hopen Radio. Since 1990 the Polish station at Hornsund and the Soviet settlements of Barentsburg and Pyramiden have each had a Norwegian sub post office run by Polish or Soviet staff but using Norwegian stamps, an internationally unique situation. Each use their own symbolic animal on their stamps (Longyearbyen: reindeer, Ny Ålesund: seal, Isfjord Radio: polar bear, Svea: musk ox, Bjørnøya Radio: guillemot, Hornsund: little auk). A curiosity for stamp collectors.

Postcards, posters and slides

There is a great variety of postcards available at Longyearbyen from the museum, Svalbardbutikken, post office, kiosk (7), community centre (4), with about 80 different scenes. Some coloured posters of Svalbard are on sale. A nice souvenir is, for instance, the official 'They attack without warning' polar bear instruction poster. A few slide series are available. Also available in Ny Ålesund, Svea and the Norwegian stations.

Radio communications

Licences are required for all transmitters and operators. Details can be obtained from the Telecommunications Administration Postboks 6701, St Olavs-Plass, N-0165 Oslo. No fee. CB is not of great use in the mountainous terrain, except within a small group, as their range is too limited. Accordingly these frequencies are not monitored by the authorities or rescue service.

Registration

All those leaving Longyearbyen on tour must register themselves and their special equipment, mode of transport, expected route and length of tour. This is to facilitate any rescue operation which might be necessary. Tour operators are responsible for the registration of their participants; others should register with the police at the airport (itinerary changes can be made at the Governor's office (2)). The police must be informed of returns to Longyearbyen and departures from Spitsbergen. Presently a new set of rules for tourism outside the settlements is in preparation that may require approval of routes and for insurance search and rescue costs from tour operators and independent visitors, in addition to the registration.

Restaurants

There is one restaurant in Huset (7), Longyearbyen, which has two rooms, one exclusively for those appropriately dressed. Two special evenings per week — *reker-aften* (shrimps) and *pizza-aften* — include a free second course. A disco is organized on Saturday nights. In the Lompen building (16) in Lia the cafeteria of the mining company also serves good meals at low (by Norwegian standard) cost and during most of the day. Snacks are also available as in the private restaurant. Alcohol is offered only in the restaurant — cheaper than on the Norwegian mainland, but still expensive. There are plans to serve alcohol also in the cafeteria in the future. In Nybyen there is a breakfast room next to reception (9) for guests of the accommodation buildings (10). The *Funken* accommodation in Haugen (10) has a dining room.

The planned hotel (21) will operate a restaurant from 1992.

A canteen is available in Barentsburg and in Pyramiden, with good meals but quite high prices (1990): breakfast 80.-nkr, lunch 110.-nkr, evening meal 110.-nkr, non-alcoholic drinks included.

Rubbish

Any disposal of waste in the field is forbidden. Litter that cannot be burned must be taken back to the settlements. Hiding litter under stones or attempting to dig holes is not a solution as frost movements soon bring it to the surface again.

At Longyearbyen all waste is dumped near the shore then covered by a layer of earth, in the hope that it will be sealed in the permafrost after a few years. There are plans for a less wasteful solution so that materials can be recycled where possible. Householders will be asked to separate their rubbish into containers for this purpose. A special leaflet on the topic of litter is available free at the airport, campsite and Governor's office.

Shopping

In the past, goods were ordered through the mining companies and surplus offered for sale to visitors. A few shops are now established in Longyearbyen. Svalbardbutikken (8) is a general store intending to move to Lia (15) probably around 1996. A shop in the entrance of Kafe Busen, Lompen (16) stocks fresh food. In summer 1990 the former food supply services (Proviantlager) for the locals was transformed into a normal shop (24), now called Provianten. Hardware can be bought at the Material-lager next to the pier and from

Yamaha and Polaris (22), which also sell motor vehicles, working clothes, etc.

Skinnboden (23), closer to the pier, specialises in clothing, skins and leather products, knives, various souvenirs, postcards, books, slides, etc. — displayed on shelves made of local driftwood. This shop also accepts British pounds, Deutsche Mark, French francs and US dollars. There are plans for Skinnboden to move close to Yamaha and Polaris.

In the building of the post office and bank, a florist has opened her shop Isrosen in 1990 on the second floor, later joined by two ladies who sell knitted articles and safety equipment for children.

The kiosk in Huset (7) stocks sweets and magazines etc. Alcoholic beverages can be bought at Norpolet in the cellar of the Funken building (10) in Haugen, open a few hours on Thursdays. Permits can be obtained from the Governor's office for strong liquor. There are enough basic supplies for visitors who plan to stay in Longyearbyen but for long tours away from the settlements it is still recommended to bring all you require.

Ny Ålesund has a kiosk and souvenir shop and Svea has a small kiosk — opening times in both settlements may be limited and not necessarily every working day. In Barentsburg there is a souvenir kiosk and usually locals selling souvenirs whenever a tourist ship is at the pier.

Show mine
Part of Mine 3 in Longyearbyen is open to the public and short tours of ½ hr (200.-nkr) and longer 2-2½ hrs (300.-nkr) are arranged. The tours give a vivid impression of a modern coal mine in Arctic conditions.

Smoking
Smoking is not allowed in any public buildings including the airport. Restaurants have smoking sections.

Sports facilities
Surprisingly, Longyearbyen offers visitors a number of possibilities for sports:
* a simple golf course without maintenance — at the old airport in the Adventdalen
* horse riding (see *horse riding*)
* shooting range in the upper Longyear valley at the bottom of Sarkophagen mountain (please set up the red flat while practising there)
* the Surf Club rents out boards and suits to visitors in summer.

Status of Svalbard
Due to the Svalbard treaty, Svalbard cannot be wholly integrated as part of Norway in spite of Norwegian sovereignty. It is directly administered from Norway and the government's representative is the *Sysselmannen pa Svalbard*. There are no locally elected political institutions except for the Svalbard council which is elected by Norwegian residents and which has a mainly consultative function.

Not all laws apply both to Norway and Svalbard. Maximum income tax, for instance, is only 10%, being the amount considered necessary for administrative purposes.

Swimming
The school's swimming pool (12) and sauna is open to visitors on most days.

Barentsburg has a 25m pool and children's pool maintained at about 27°C, open every day except Mondays. Pyramiden also has a pool (the most northerly).

With all these possibilities, even if you have no intention of bathing from the pretty beaches, you should come prepared for an Arctic swim!

Sysselmann

The Governor's office (2) is a modern building with a dark wooden facing and dark grey roof. It is the only permanent police station and main administrative office. The Sysselmann of Svalbard is a unique institution in Norway (except for a period in the '30s when Norway tried to annex part of Greenland and install a governor there too). He is chosen by the elected government and appointed by the King of Norway, not only representative of Norway but chief of police and rescue services and in charge of low level jurisdiction. The Governor's term in office is limited to a few years.

Telecommunications

Svalbard is now linked via satellite to world wide telecommunication networks. Direct dialling is possible to most destinations. To mainland Norway a 0 is used before the city code, 095 enters the international network followed by the usual country code. There are less reliable coin operated telephones at the airport, campsite, post-office, *Kafe busen* (16) and *Huset* (7) or, in preference, calls can be made from the telecommunications office (3) in Longyearbyen (open until 15.30 Mondays to Fridays) where payment is made after the call without the problem of having to have the correct coins available. At the office fax and telex messages can also be sent and received.

Telephones are installed at all other settlements and at the Norwegian weather stations.

Traffic to and from Spitsbergen

Apart from cruise ships the only regular access to the islands is on flights from Tromsø and Oslo. Braathens S.A.F.E. and SAS serve these routes with up to six flights per week. Compared to other routes of comparable length the flights are expensive. In summer they are generally booked well in advance. The Soviets have regular fortnightly flights from Murmansk.

Since the daily ship service along the Norwegian mainland (Hurtigrute) ceased operations in Spitsbergen all freight comes by ship from Bodo; passengers are not allowed. All excess baggage comes either via Bodo by sea or as air cargo at a more expensive rate. Any excess equipment required during a stay should be sent well in advance. Remember that supply ships can only sail during the ice-free period (usually end of May to early December). At other times air transport is the only alternative. Only on the journey from the mainland at the start of the summer season (June) and at its end (late August) is there occasionally a chance of a berth on these freight ships.

See also *Internal Traffic*.

Bibliography

Conway, Sir Martin. *No Man's Land*, Cambridge 1906

Gjoerevoll, Røenning. *Flowers of Svalbard*, Oslo 1980

Greve, T. Svalbard. *Norway in the Arctic*, Oslo 1975

Hisdal, Vidar. *Geography of Svalbard*, Oslo 2nd edition 1985

Larsen, Thor. 'Polar Bear, Lonely Nomad of the North', *National Geographic* Vol 139 No 4, 4/1971, p. 5745-590

Lövenskiold, H.L. *Avifauna Svalbardensis*, Oslo 1963

Maclean, Alistair. *Bear Island*, London 1971

Mathisen, Trygve. *Svalbard in International Politics 1871-1925*, Oslo 1954

— *Svalbard in the changing Arctic*, Oslo 1954

Mehlum, Fridtjov. *Birds and Mammals of Svalbard*, Oslo 1989.

Norsk Sjøkartsverk. *Arctic Pilot*, Volume 7 Svalbard-Jan Mayen 1988

Østreng, W. *Politics in high latitudes. The Svalbard archipelago*. London 1977

— *Svalbard, The Islands of Peace*, Norway 1987

Worsley/Statoil. *The Geological History of Svalbard*, Stavanger 1988

MAPS

There is a comprehensive range of maps available, all of which are continuously updated. As there are only a few sheets produced each year, it may take some time before a particular map is brought up to date; some are quite out of date and unreliable as far as glaciers, watercourses, and coastlines are concerned. This is already covered in the section on the geography of Spitsbergen.

A list of maps available in Britain can be obtained from Stanfords (12-14 Long Acre, Covent Garden, London WC2E 9LP, Tel. 071-836 1321).

The following are usually available:

Comprehensive map — physical   1: 2,000,000

Comprehensive map — physical   1: 1,000,000

Comprehensive map — physical, four sheets 1: 500,000

Area map — physical (Nordenskiøldland)   1: 200,000

Coastal map   1: 200,000
Will eventually comprise 14 sheets, so far three are available. They are sheet A3 (Kongsfjord to the western Isfjord) sheet B4 (southern Nordenskiøldland to the northern side of Hornsund) and B5 (Hornsund to South Cape).

Comprehensive map — physical (62 sheets) 1: 100,000

Area map Bear Island   1: 50,000

The maps to a scale of 1:100,000 are suitable for walkers only for general orientation. They are available in three editions, one in colour and two in black and white. The latter are being gradually replaced by the superior coloured series. The maps covering the area from South Cape (Sørkapp) north to the northern shore of Isfjord and along the western coast to Krossfjord have been published in colour; some of the maps have however not been updated since the late '40s. All other sheets are still in black and white. It is quite common to find maps are temporarily unavailable.

For those interested in geology there are several specialist maps currently available. A booklet in English accompanies these maps.

Comprehensive map — geological   1: 1,000,000

Comprehensive map — geological
(four sheets)   1: 500,000

Area map - geological   1: 250,000
(Northern and central part of Nordaustlandet)

Comprehensive map — geological   1: 100,000
Will comprise 62 sheets, but so far only four (B1OG Van Mijenfjorden, C8G Billefjorden, C9G Adventdalen and C10G Braganzavagen) have been published; in numbers and areas covered they will correspond to the map series — physical.

Area maps — geomorphological   1: 50,000
Brøgger-Peninsula (Ny Ålesund), no accompanying booklet, text in French.

There are also available a few specialist maps on vegetation, covering limited areas.

Photographs

Selected pictures by Andreas Umbreit:

Slide series (6 slides per set, each set 12.-DM plus postage and package:

* Svalbard: The Five Settlements (late 1990)
* Svalbard: Coastal Landscapes (late 1990)
* Svalbard: Inland Landscapes (early 1991)
* Svalbard: The Forces of Ice and Frost (late 1991)
* Fauna of Svalbard (Birds (late 1991)
* Fauna of Svalbard: Mammals (late 1991)
* Flora of Svalbard I (early 1992)
* Flora of Svalbard II (early 1992)

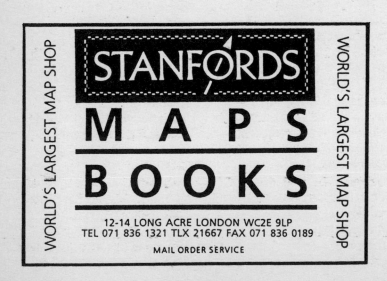

INDEX

Windsurfing near Longyearbyen. With the water just above freezing this is an unexpected Spitsbergen sport.

NOTES

NOTES

NOTES

NOTES